UNDERSTANDING WOODCARVING

The best from WOODCarving *magazine*

UNDERSTANDING
WOODCARVING

The best from **WOODCarving** *magazine*

GUILD OF MASTER CRAFTSMAN PUBLICATIONS LTD

This collection first published in 1997 by
Guild of Master Craftsman Publications Ltd,
Castle Place, 166 High Street, Lewes, East Sussex BN7 1XU

ISBN 1 86108 045 X

Printed and bound in Hong Kong by
Dai Nippon Printing Company.

Front cover photograph supplied by John Hoyle

Back cover photograph supplied by Peter Tree

CONTENTS

NOTES

Please note that names, addresses, prices etc were correct at the time the articles were originally published, but may since have changed.

MEASUREMENTS

Throughout the book instances will be found where a metric measurement has fractionally varying imperial equivalents, usually within $\frac{1}{16}$in either way. This is because in each particular case the closest imperial equivalent has been given. A mixture of metric and imperial measurements should NEVER be used – always use either one or the other.

INTRODUCTION

To the uninitiated woodcarving is a mystery. The transformation of a log or a plain piece of wood into a facsimile of a familiar article or concept is to be wondered at and admired. The deeper you explore the craft, the more questions need answers and, as each piece of wood is unique, there are always new questions.

Most people imagine woodcarving is a craft practised by a few wizened old craftsmen in dusty workshops. But even the slightest investigation reveals that woodcarving is a broad and vital subject. It ranges from the whittling of simple figures, through monumental sculptures, to applied domestic decoration. It is practised by all ages, races and sexes.

The way carvers work depends on their personal choice of tools and their imagination. Some prefer hand tools alone and have as much interest in the process of carving as in the finished object. Others are more concerned with the finished carving, and less interested in how they arrive at it.

The majority fit between these extremes, using a variety of tools and techniques and allowing features in the wood some influence on the finished carving. In the past carvers had only their chisels and gouges, now power tools have added new possibilities. Wood can be carved more thinly and with more detail than ever before.

This book is made up of articles selected from *Woodcarving* magazine to show some of the more complex methods of work. Experienced carvers both amateur and professional show what they do and why.

Here you will find the reason people carve – as a career or for pleasure. The subjects and style they choose – detailed lifelike representation or stylised abstraction. The choice of woods – straight-grained or highly figured, soft or hard. The tools used – power tools or chisels and gouges.

Techniques are explained and, just as important, the reasoning behind them and how this affects the finished carving. I hope it will help you to appreciate both the art and craft of woodcarving.

Neil Bell
Managing Editor, *Woodcarving*

FEATURE PLEASU

S uccess! What a wonderful word. Recently, I spoke to two ex-businessmen from very different backgrounds, with a very different approach to their carving, and it was some time before I realised the outstanding attribute they have in common – success. One carves as a hobby and the other as a business, but since they both started less than three years ago, people have been queuing up to buy their work.

Frank Hayward's hobby left him with few places at home to display his pieces. His wife, in desperation, persuaded him to exhibit them. In just two shows he sold nearly every piece and was turning down commissions because he does not create pieces for sale, or want the commitment of other people's deadlines.

Chris Manley takes a different view. After only one or two carvings, he was receiving commissions from local customers and keen galleries, and admits it is definitely a business for him. "If I don't work we don't eat. It is our only source of income," he told me.

So, while Frank spends hours putting realistic detail into half an inch for the love of it, Chris will work out the amount of detail necessary to create vitality in a piece, but within defined time and cost constraints. Talking to them both, I discovered the common denominators to their success were application, dedication, training and research.

Business enterprise

On the fringe of Egdon Heath, buried down the Dorset lanes and hidden in the old buildings of a farm in Dorset, Chris runs his business, helped by craftsman Toby House.

In a large white-washed workshop, which used to be a cattleshed, Chris works business-like hours and keeps timesheets on his carvings, so they can be priced accordingly.

He carves mainly wildlife, although I did spot a fascinating female torso, lurking on top of a cupboard in his workshop. A journalist who writes profiles on famous actors warned me the canny ones refused to be interviewed in their own homes because too much information could be gleaned. Beware, carvers, of your workshops!

Chris aims to produce simple but recognisable shapes in nice woods, polished to create a pleasing effect. They are the kind of silhouettes you could cut out and ask children to identify. He had a motley collection of woods under his bench and the finished carvings I saw were from diverse timbers, from lacewood (*Platanus hybrida*), to local Weymouth pine (*Pinus strobus*) and laburnum (*laburnum vulgare*), to blackened ironbark from his sister's barbecue in Australia.

He tries to match the wood to the subject and demonstrates this with a black stripe through the eye of a nuthatch and the fur impression of lacewood grain on a bear's tummy.

He sometimes buys wood from Bill Wilder in Wiltshire or simply uses timber from his own backyard woodlands. He spoke enthusiastically of a black walnut tree (*Juglans nigra*) he got after a big storm. It was 2m, 6½ft thick and dried out beautifully.

Repeat work

We talked about customers wanting the piece you have just sold and the issues involved in repeating carvings. One man at a show had just offered Chris twice the price to carve another large runner duck, which he had already sold, but he refused.

Some of Chris' pieces are unique but some are repeated, although every piece comes out differently, and not just because of the different wood. Chris believes each time you do a carving you get a better one. He showed me a cheetah, which he said had improved and developed.

This animal had to be stretched to give the impression

Right **Kestrel in elm (*Ulmus spp*) by Chris Manley**
Far right **Cheetah by Chris Manley**

Below from left to right
● **Runner duck by Chris Manley**
● **Wren in iron bark by Chris Manley**
● **Chris shows off his carving of a locally caught salmon**
● **Chris Manley's bear is in lacewood**

RE AND PROFIT

of speed, the legs grouped together to look fast, and the whole design had to be strong enough not to break. He found a pose which worked and pointed out the small changes he made from the original, such as chest depth and leg position. He continues to produce cheetahs because there is a good market for them.

I admire his honesty and wonder if it really matters whether an artist produces similar pieces. Chris has never used anyone else's patterns or 'how to' books. Here is a man who is not letting the work become boring and sloppy, he is re-thinking and re-working the piece, which is an opportunity few of us have.

Time management

Chris admitted he used power tools to do the time-consuming roughing out. This saves time for Toby, who works on the repetitive tasks such as roughing out and sanding. More time is spent on sanding than anything else, and half Toby's time is spent on the wet and dry.

Chris enjoys the freedom to design, plan, sketch and develop new pieces. Pieces don't get faster, they get better he says.

Pricing work is a common problem for carvers and there is a limit on what you can ask for most pieces. So he works out carefully the amount of detail worth adding and how much fiddling will pay, as it's always tempting to carry on adding detail.

Pieces don't get faster, they get better

Torso in Chris' workshop

Often, I receive enquiries from carvers who, after being made redundant or retiring early, want to know if carving could be a good job or business proposition. It is rather like the chicken and egg question. There are so many imponderables, such as how hard you are prepared to work, how business-like, flexible and organised you are.

You are often asked at interviews, "What makes you think you could do this job successfully?" Chris might be someone who could answer this. He has managed several fish farms, and developed business experience. He completed three courses in natural history and technical illustration, and has a drawing ability I envy. He used a lathe at school and has enjoyed learning about different woods. Add enthusiasm and determination and you have success.

Confident cuts

He took up the government's enterprise allowance scheme to get through his first year and the course made him study the business approach to marketing his work. He knew how difficult it was to sell two-dimensional work but found a market for his first simple chainsaw carvings.

He started in the garden with a chainsaw and then a Hegner power carver. He bought a tree for £15 and cut out a heron. Two branches were left over from which he carved the female torso in his workshop. His second carving was a full-size salmon (34½ lbs) which was caught in the local river. Next, he was commissioned to carve a cheetah, then a lion, and more people started buying.

Chris soon discovered people loved wildlife and wood as much as he did, and with his training he had no trouble designing patterns. I was amazed at his ability to visualise the rest of an animal from one picture. His college training taught him to draw the back of an object when seeing only the front, and his drawings show more than the simplistic shape of his finished carving. They show the bones and construction of the animal.

If you really know the shape and contours you can cut with confidence and achieve the original image you visualised. The amount of detail on the surface is unimportant, because you have achieved the story of the piece through simple contours, and secondly, the grain in the wood has been chosen to contribute to the character. He is, he says, a three dimensional illustrator working in wood, rather than a carver.

Top **Female sparrohawk (1994) by Frank Hayward**
Above **Frank Hayward in his workshop**

This is a man who likes to get things right and to win competitions

Labour of love

In sharp contrast to Chris Manley, Frank Hayward carves birds in a detailed or decorative style, spending hours and hours on a few square inches. There are no time limits or customer constraints, as he carves only to please himself.

Three years ago, Frank grew prize-winning orchids and played golf. He still plays golf which he loves, but now carves, reads about carving, researches the birds and then carves again. Like so many retired people, he wonders how he ever had time to work.

He was first employed as a joiner in 1936, and retired six years ago from the building firm he started with his brother. While travelling in New England, he came across specialist bird carving shops and was amazed at the quality and prices. On his return, he leafed through all his old woodworking magazines and found an article by David Clews on bird carving, with a picture of a ¾ size teal duck.

He followed the pattern with a knife he made himself, using 1in, 25mm obeche (*Triplochiton scleroxylon*), which he had laminated to make it the right size. Pleased with the result, he sent for a Pintail Decoy Supplies catalogue so he could do something else. He had accumulated some tools already and knew how to glue wood up without showing the joins.

First, he started with his bird in a vice and hacked with an axe and rasp, and finally with a knife. He has used gouges and mallets since, but found they were difficult when carving a songbird. He liked to hold the bird in his hands.

Frank decided to buy some power tools quite early on because "if you're going to do a job you need the tools to do it". He bought a cheap electric hand-drill with a flexible shaft handpiece and after ten minutes it was too hot, so he bought the proper machinery. "I don't class myself as a carver, more of a sculptor with these tools," he remarked. But power tools are also helpful to his shoulder which was damaged during his army service.

Studying pays

Frank bought books and videos, and then commuted between the lounge and the garden workshop, putting the advice in his head straight into action. For the first 12 months he was on his own, but then discovered another bird carver at a local RSPB show at Gillingham and then found the local group of the British Decoy and Wildfowl Carving Association.

I remember clearly Frank's first visit to our group, as he absorbed advice and information like a sponge. Then he collected appropriate study birds, both taxidermists' mounts and resin castings of work by champion American carvers.

There are some carvers who are determined to improve and Frank is unstoppable. This is a man who likes to get things right and to win competitions. With 16 entries to three carving competitions, he won 13 ribbons, four of which were first places. The first year he was prevented from entering Novice level and was promoted to Intermediate, which he then won.

Frank put his progress down to reading and practising instead of watching television. His eyes were on the next competition, as he liked to see what others were doing and to try to judge his work against theirs.

Successful shows

By this stage he had accumulated a lot of birds and his house was filling up. He sold his first birds at the East of England Exhibition at Pensthorpe in 1993. On the first day six

Above **This Hen Canuasback illustrates Frank Hayward's superb featherwork**
Left **Male American kestrel by Frank Hayward**

Above **Mandarin by
Frank Hayward**
Left **Kestrel by
Frank Hayward**
Right **Kingfisher
by Frank Hayward**

carvings were sold and four of them were Frank's. He hadn't a clue what price to put on them but tried to make it realistic.

They had been sitting on top of a cabinet at home, "virtually the only place my wife will have them," said Frank. Although she loved to have the birds around the house Frank's prolific carving made it a matter of space.

By 1994 the number of birds was growing rapidly, so he entered eight carvings into the Pensthorpe National Show and sold seven. There are now many people eagerly awaiting Frank's entries to the next show.

The most difficult skill to acquire was painting, and Frank has an added difficulty with balancing the brush, as he lost most of his right little finger on a planer. He has used instructional books on how to mix colours, and followed USA champion carver Jim Sprankle's advice on a course and in his book, but still asked me if it was possible to copy natural feathers with paint.

"I don't think you can do it. A lot can be achieved but you have to give and take a bit," he admitted. This was an unusual statement from this determined man. He has achieved a great deal in three years but he does not give and take a bit, he really enjoys getting it right. ●

TILLER TYPES

DEREK OLDBURY TELLS HOW HE CARVED SOME SMALL REPLICA RUDDERHEADS

Above left **Group of rudderheads**
Above **Maiden's head in a crocodile's jaws, with its gilded young on its head**
Far left **Merchant in red and gilt**
Left **Naval officer in blue and gilt**

heads mounted on bows, but other parts were equally adorned. Mastheads, stern boards and rudder blades were all decorated with relief carvings.

RUDDER REPLICAS

The most original and eccentric carvings, however, were those on the stock of the rudder. Mythical animals and allegorical figures arose from the superstitious ideas of the carvers.

I have carved several small scale replicas of some of these allegorical figures, which I coloured with paint and gilt. Inspiration came from illustrations in the book *Art And The Seafarer* edited by Hans Jurgen Hansen, published by Faber and Faber in 1968 (available in larger libraries).

The book has a small section on rudderheads, with most of the illustrations in black and white, but a few in colour.

The figures I carved were: a

Few early wooden ships have survived for us to study, but information is available in a few maritime museums around the world, including the National Maritime Museum at Greenwich.

Two famous ships which have been preserved are Nelson's Victory at Portsmouth and the Cutty Sark at Greenwich. These, and the museum records, give us some idea of the artistic

splendour of their ornamentation.

Western ships reached the peak of decorative and ornamental woodcarving during the 17th and 18th centuries. Carvings were applied to bows, sterns, masts, rudders and cabins, either for religious or superstitious reasons, or to show off the wealth of their owners.

Probably best known are the carved and lavishly decorated figure-

Top left **The tracing of the cavalier is transferred to the lime block with carbon paper and enhanced with felt tip pen**
Top centre **Cutting away the outline starts at the top of the head**
Top right **The upper face, hat and plumes are sculpted**
Left **The lower face, moustache and beard are defined but the head remains integral with the body**

I had a 4 x 4in, 100 x 100mm beam of lime which I cut into 10in, 255mm lengths, and also an 8in, 200mm cube.

I made line tracings of the illustrations in the book and then enlarged them by photocopying until they fitted the lime blocks. The tracings were transferred to the wood using a sheet of carbon paper, and then enhanced with black felt tip pen.

I had to make do with front view only from the illustrations and imagine the side view, which is easier than it seems. The exception was the crocodile maiden which had a three quarters front view. I transferred this so the carving was diagonal to the block, which made the best use of the wood.

CAVALIER

This is how I carved the replica 18th century cavalier figure. As with all the figures, I started carving at the top of the block, removing excess wood beyond the outline of the upper head, hat and hair with a variety of gouges and a medium weight lignum vitae (*Guaiacum spp*) mallet.

With only a front view and an imagined profile, I began carving from the front, allowing the nose, lips and other protruding parts like hair and hat, to rise from the surface into which the gouge was entering. I attempted to model the shape rather than get a square, cuboid look.

I next sculpted the upper face, hat and plumes, remembering the hat brim inclined upwards at the front and downwards to the left. Then I did the

merchant in a red coat and hat with a gilt crown, a maiden with her head enclosed in the jaws of a crocodile, a naval officer in navy blue with a golden cockade and moustache, a pop-eyed girl with rosy apple cheeks, an Egyptian King's head in blue and gold, and a dreamy-eyed cavalier in aubergine and yellow.

MATERIALS

Ships' decorations were characterised by eccentricity and bright colours, so I decided to use lime (*Tilia vulgaris*) which is the most carving-friendly of woods. It is strong with subtle curvilinear grain and tolerant to any direction of cutting and sculpting.

Above left **The full head is now modelled and distinct from the body**
Above right **Profile of the modelled head ready for the application of fine detail**

lower face, moustache and beard and refined the nose and mouth. At this stage the head was not clearly defined from the body.

As I continued modelling the face and further details emerged, I found myself shaping the sides too, and almost without realising it produced the basis of a suitable side elevation to complement the front.

I found it important not to be afraid of changing the gouge, both in size and curvature, during the sculpting. Also, after initial use of the mallet I changed to using both hands to grip the gouge handle for better control.

Once the initially modelled head was clearly distinct from the body it was ready for fine carving of the features and details of the hat and plumage. The face and hair were refined, the eyes incised, the neck and chest completed, and the feathering of the hat finished.

Once the carving was completed I gave the whole head a light rub down with fine grit flour paper and dusted it off with a clean cloth and brush in preparation for painting. The surface could be sealed if required and the nap rubbed away before the colour work begins.

PAINTING

I have found the best colour effect is obtained using artists' oil paints mixed with oil and spirit of turpentine to get the required degree of thinness and exact shade of colour.

Unlike colour stain, it is better to

Below left **Using a Pfeil 3mm, ⅛in U section gouge to sculpt the lower eyelid**
Below centre **The face, hair and eyes are now detailed**
Below right **Using a fine skew chisel to carve the feathering detail**

use this oilpaint and turps mixture (more turps than oil) and apply it thinly with a good quality brush. You can then add more thin coats or try dabs of stronger colour alternating with thin coats.

I started on the cavalier with a thin clear wash of aubergine over the hat and body using a large soft brush. I used yellow ochre for the vest and sash and a coat of gilt paint for the feathers and sash.

For the face I used a flesh tint touched with cherry red on the cheeks. The hair and eye pupils were black and the eye irises blue. I repeated the treatment to intensify the colours after 24 hours when the first coat had dried. This gave a bright, fairground effect.

You can play with the paint on the surface to get interesting colour diffused effects, which is preferable to a uniform slab of thick colour which disguises the presence of the wood. You should aim for a partnership, a balance of wood and colour rather than a domination of one over the other.

COLOURS

It is best to mix and use only small quantities of colour at a time and to try out the colour on an offcut of the same wood so you get an idea of what it will

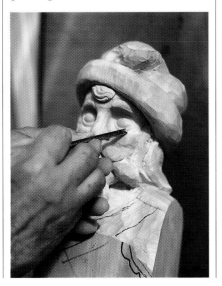

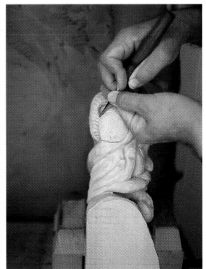

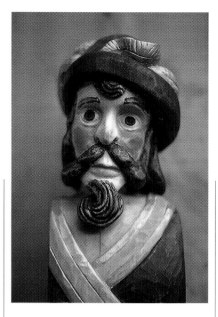

Above **The first stage of colouring produces a bright, fairground appearance**
Below **A thin wash of turps and raw umber gives an antique effect and unifies the garish colours**

look like before applying it to your carving. Keep a clean cloth and small bottle of turps handy to remove or dilute unwanted colour effects.

Try different methods of painting, sometimes allowing thin coats to dry and sometimes mixing blobs of different colour in patches here and there. Enjoy the painting and application of colour. If you have not done it before do not let uncertainty restrain you.

I finished the cavalier with a thin wash of turps and raw umber applied generously to produce an antique effect and to unify the garish colours.

There are several gilding agents available commercially, some paste-like in a tube, others consisting of gold particles in a suspension of liquid solvent. These are quite expensive but worth a try for that finishing touch. True gold leaf is even more expensive and best kept for high quality projects.

Once all the paint is thoroughly dry, you can finish the surface with a light coat of beeswax and buff it gently with a soft clean cloth.

I should emphasise that the carving is the most important part of this project. The rudderhead must be a convincing character in its own right and should stand on its own in its natural state. It must not rely on the painting for its effectiveness. Rather, the colouring is an added bonus which complements the excellence of the carving, and is not a cover-up for carving defects.

Always aim for excellence in your carving and avoid slipshod methods which give carving a bad name. Do your best work on every piece and the bonus is yours, the joy of carving. ●

Derek Oldbury was an engineer and scientist as well as lecturer at Luton University for 24 years before he took early retirement and moved to St Ives, Cornwall eight years ago. He took up carving about 20 years ago as an antidote to academic work and now teaches adult education classes in carving. He also has a space in a local craft market where he takes commissions.

IN THE FRAME

RAY WINDER EXPLAINS HOW TO MAKE AN ART NOUVEAU STYLE FRAME

I used five woodcarving chisels for this project. They were a 10mm, ⅜in V tool; 13mm, ½in No.3 fishtail gouge; 7mm, ¼in No.8 gouge; 4mm, ³⁄₁₆in No.8 and a 5mm No.3. If you find other chisel sizes more convenient and they do the job that's fine. You will need a router to cut the recess on the back of the frame.

I used a block of lime (*Tilia vulgaris*) with dimensions 10 x 12¾ x 1¼in, 255 x 324 x 32mm. You could use North American basswood (*Tilia americana*) which is very similar, and both woods can be stained to give a darker finish. For the more ambitious, a naturally darker and more attractive wood such as cherry (*Prunus spp*) or walnut (*Juglans spp*) will repay the extra effort needed to carve it.

Having prepared the wood to the correct thickness (1¼in, 32mm), trace the outline and other details of the frame from your plans or drawings using carbon paper. You can draw the plans yourself, but if you are less experienced or lack confidence, detailed plans are available from me (see the end of this article).

Next, cut around the outline using either a bandsaw or an electric jigsaw. The hatched areas shown in the picture can be removed later.

Below left **The outline of the frame is traced onto the prepared wood and the outline is cut out using a bandsaw or electric jigsaw**
Below **A recess is cut in the back of the frame**

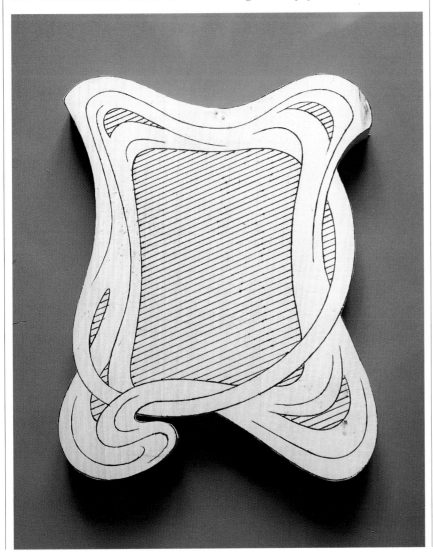

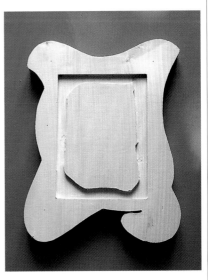

Now turn over the frame and mark the outline of a recess as shown. Using a router, cut to a depth of 6mm. It is not necessary to recess the whole area as most of it will be cut away.

WASTE REMOVAL

Returning to the front of the frame, cut out the hatched area of waste. Drill out as much as possible and then clean up the edges with a chisel or electric jigsaw.

Instead of using clumsy clamps to hold the wood down while carving, I used an 18mm, ⅝in MDF scrap of wood which was cut to fit the recess. This was carefully screwed in place, taking care that the screws penetrated

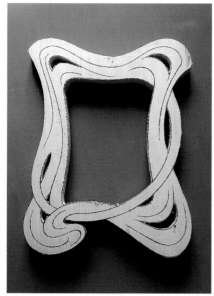 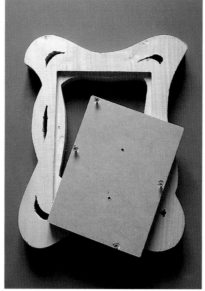 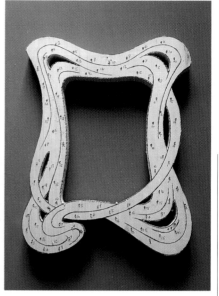

not more than about 6mm, ¼in into the
frame. The best positions for the screws
are shown on the photograph of the
back of the frame.

You can now trace depth guide
marks and their measurements onto
the wood. They need to be carefully
drilled using a small bit, ideally around
2mm, ⅟₁₆in diameter. A bench drill with
a depth gauge is the easiest method,
although a hand-held drill can be used
by marking each required depth on the
drill bit with a piece of tape.
Remember, it's better to drill the hole a
little less than required than too deep.

The measurements marked beside
the holes are useful guides to the depth
of adjacent holes and help determine
the sequence for carving certain areas.

FRAME FRONT

Starting with the bottom part of the
frame, make the first cuts with the V
tool. Start cutting down either side of
the lines which mark the curve of the
limb growing out of the left hand side
of the frame, continuing down first
under one corner and then over the
right hand corner to disappear up
behind the top right corner. As the
frame only needs to be carved into

areas of flat planes at this stage, a
13mm, ½in No.3 fishtail chisel is ideal.

Lower the areas on each side of the
limb by cutting up to the V tool chisel
cuts, using the drilled holes as
reference points to show you when to
stop carving. If you make some small
crosses where a hole has or is about to
disappear, they will provide reference
points later for re-drawing details on
the wood. With the sides lowered, the
parts of the limb which pass behind or
under the other parts of the frame can
be carved to the pre-drilled depths.

Next, the areas linking the four
corners can be carved, cutting down to
the shallowest holes first and marking

crosses as you go. By checking your
plans, and using the crosses and holes
as a guide, you can re-draw onto the
wood the original lines which you have
carved away.

Moving to the top of the frame and
using the re-drawn lines as a guide, use
the 7mm, ¼in No.8 chisel to define the
furrows which curve along and around
the inner rim. Always work from the
highest spots down to the lower ones,
re-drawing the guidelines as you carve
them away. You can also round over
the top edge slightly with the fishtail.

Next, the bottom corners can be
carved in more detail using the 7mm, ¼in
No.8, following the guide lines and drilled
holes as in the previous
stage. The outer edges
of these corners can be
rounded over ready for
the next stage.

BACK WORK

Moving to the back of
the frame, you can still
use your scrap of
wood as a holding
piece, but it will need
a holding block
screwed to the front
side to raise the frame
clear of the bench, or
hold it in a vice.

You will reach a
point where this
holding piece must be
removed to carve
behind the section of
the limb which passes
across the corner. The

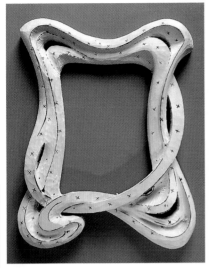 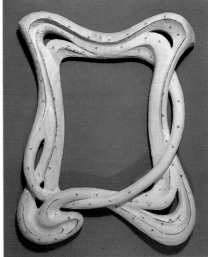

frame can be held down while this part is carved by laying a packing piece across the back of the frame and clamping it down, taking care not to use excessive pressure.

As with the initial stages of carving the frame front, the first cuts should form flat planes using the fishtail chisel. Study these pictures to determine where the wood needs to be cut away to give the impression the limb weaves under and over the parts of the frame which you have already carved.

You do not need to drill holes on the back, as the depth of the carving on the front will dictate how much to cut away on the back.

Once the rear of the frame has been finished, and all the edges

Above left **The outer edges of the corners can be rounded over**
Above **Define the furrows and edges of the frame front**
Below **The finished art nouveau style frame**

rounded and ready for sanding, the front can be finished.

FINAL CUTS

Use the 7mm, ¼in No.8 gouge to define more fully the furrow which sweeps from the top left hand corner, right down the left hand side to the lower corner.

Then you can use the 4mm, ⅜in No.8 gouge to further define the furrows and edges. Round over the square edges of the limb, taking care to

keep it a smooth, flowing shape. There are lots of awkward corners which need to be cleaned up. A 5mm, ⅜in No.3 is useful here as is a scalpel for fine undercutting.

The better the finish you achieve direct from the tool, the easier the sanding will be later. A small burr in a high speed hand piece is excellent for cleaning up some of the deeper areas in the corners.

The frame needs to be very finely finished if you want to achieve a smooth flowing surface. This requires care and patience when sanding.

I started with 100 grit cloth-backed abrasive, working through finer grades to finish with 600 grit for a silky-smooth finish. Folding or rolling the abrasive is useful for getting into awkward areas, as is sticking pieces to flat or shaped sticks. But be careful not to sand crisp edges away.

When you have got an entirely scratch-free surface, seal the wood with either a sanding sealer or several coats of matt varnish thinned 60/40 with white spirit and wiped on and off with a cloth to avoid heavy build up. Sand lightly between coats before finally finishing with wax polish.

Use a piece of hardboard or wood of a similar thickness for the back. This together with a 2mm, ⅜in picture glass or mirror can be held in place with little hardwood (oak, or an equally strong wood) toggles screwed in place. Small brass ones are available for picture frames for a much neater finish. If you decide to make a hinged stand, it is best to make it from a stronger wood. ●

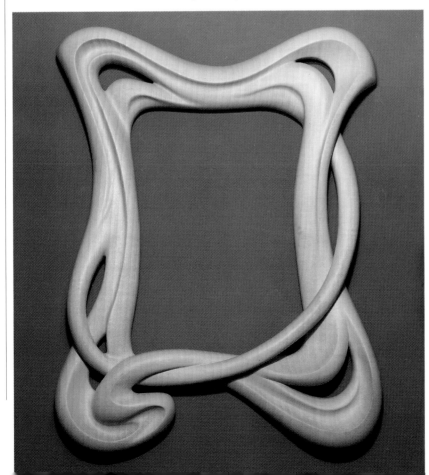

A full set of plans, including designs for a frame stand and hinge, is available from Ray Winder for £7.00. For further details of his other woodcarving projects contact Ray Winder at The Old Granary, Mercers Farm, Nutfield Marsh Road, Nutfield, Surrey RH1 4EU
Tel: 01737 643951

BRANCHING OUT

MICHEL THERIAULT DESCRIBES HOW TO MAKE AN UNUSUAL TREE MIRROR FRAME

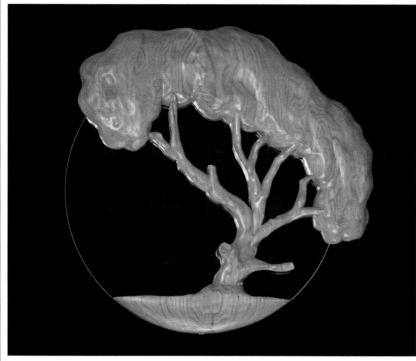

This pierced relief carving is an ideal project for both the experienced carver looking for a practical application of their skills, and the beginner looking for an achievable yet useful project.

The carving is straightforward using simple carving tools, and the details are easy to accomplish. Hanging in a front hallway or entrance, this carving is certain to be looked at regularly.

I chose butternut (or white walnut, *Juglans cinera*) for this carving, but other walnuts (*Juglans spp.*) would also be a good choice, keeping in mind the wood you choose should fit in well with the other elements of a room.

Butternut is a popular wood for carving, as it is quite soft yet has an attractive grain, ideal for natural finished carvings. This carving is glued up from dressed 2in x 6in x 5ft, 50mm x 150mm x 1.5m long board. The finished dimensions are 1½ x 5¼in, 38 x 135mm.

Above **The finished tree mirror.**
Below **The blank is clamped.**

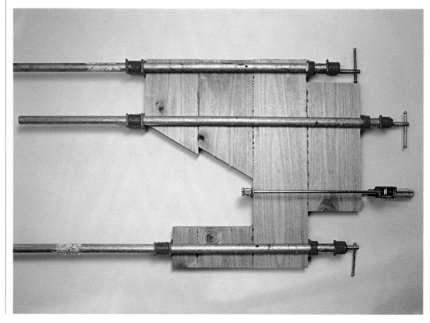

An 18in, 460mm diameter ³⁄₁₆in, 5mm thick mirror with a bronze tint forms the backdrop for the tree carving. The bronze tint provides a much warmer reflection than the standard silver and compliments the wood nicely. Make sure you get the edges polished to prevent cuts, since the edges will be exposed.

Standard metal mirror clips and picture wire are used to attach the mirror to the carving and to hang it on the wall. You will need to bend one of the mirror clips to hold the mirror at the bottom of the tree carving.

THE BLANK

The first step is to produce a full size pattern from the one given. You have a couple of options for this, the easiest being to use a photocopier to enlarge the pattern in sections.

If you don't have access to a photocopier, you can use grid lines to reproduce it onto graph paper. If necessary, tape together sheets of paper to make the required size.

Before you begin copying the pattern, draw an 18in, 460mm diameter circle to represent the

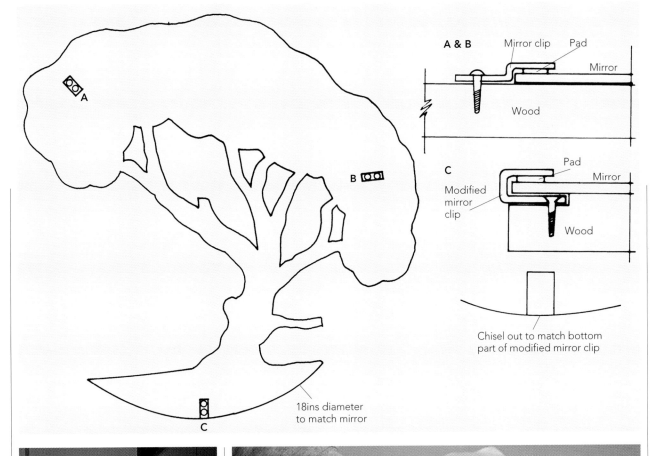

A & B Mirror clip Pad
Mirror
Wood

C Pad
Mirror
Modified mirror clip
Wood

Chisel out to match bottom part of modified mirror clip

18ins diameter to match mirror

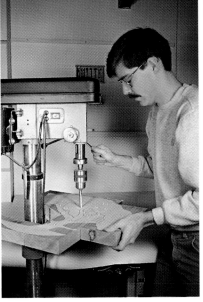

Michel drills holes in the blank between branches for threading the fret saw blade through to cut out the waste.

....

location of the mirror, and use it as a reference point. Once you have made your pattern, you can either use it as is, or trace it onto a sheet of tracing paper to preserve your first pattern.

Cut the board carefully to get the most efficient use of your wood. Using the pattern to ensure the pieces are lined up properly, glue the pieces

together and clamp.

If you don't have enough clamps to do the whole piece together, glue it up in sections. Remember to use a scrap piece of softwood between your clamp and the blank to avoid denting the soft wood, which could show through as a gap when you glue the next piece on.

Once the entire blank is dry, glue the pattern to the blank using a spray adhesive (available at most arts and crafts supply stores). Follow the

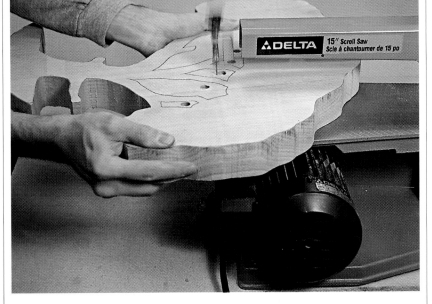

Using a scroll saw to cut the waste out from between the branches.

....

instructions on the can for a temporary bond so you can easily remove the pattern after cutting.

Next, cut out the blank to the outside of the lines. A bandsaw will work for most of the outside of the tree, but you will need to use a fretsaw, scroll saw or jigsaw for the interior cut-outs. If you don't have a bandsaw you could use a fretsaw or padsaw for the

Using a mallet and ¾in, 20mm carpenters chisel to knock the edges off the tree canopy and rough out the canopy edges.

Smoothing the surface of the tree canopy with a ¾in, 20mm chisel.

outline, and drill out the openings. For the interior, drill a hole large enough to start the cut with the blade you are using with each interior cut-out.

The fretsaw will give you a fairly smooth cut, but will be somewhat slow, even if you use an aggressive skip tooth blade. With a jigsaw, make sure your blade can manage the 1½in, 38mm thickness and use a fine tooth blade. When cutting, take care at the bottom of the tree where the radius matches that of the mirror to ensure it stays accurate.

ROUGHING OUT

Now you have a blank to work with, the next step is to rough out the details. A regular ¾in, 20mm carpenters chisel is ideal for most of the work. However you will also need a ½in, 13mm No 6 gouge to work the valleys in the tree canopy surface, and a carving knife to do some of the work on the limbs and branches.

When carving butternut, it is particularly important to make sure your carving tools are very sharp, so hone and strop them before you begin and frequently strop them while you are working. It is amazing how quickly you get used to dull tools and how surprisingly easier it is to work with them after they have been sharpened.

Before carving, lay the blank face up on a large piece of plywood, which will serve as a carving platform and save your workbench from stray cuts. You can simply clamp the blank down, or screw the blank onto the plywood from underneath and then clamp the

plywood directly to your bench to keep the blank secure while carving.

You may need to rotate the board as you carve for the easiest carving position. Always keep in mind the direction of the grain as you cut so you don't accidentally chip out a large piece.

Start shaping the tree canopy. Using solid cuts, either by hand or with the help of a mallet, knock off the edges to round the canopy then work with the grain to develop a pleasing shape. Remember the surface should not be completely smooth and uniform, but should have hills and valleys to represent the branches and leaves.

You can use a photograph of trees as an example, or do what looks right to you. Better still look at real trees.

Every once in a while, you should set the blank upright and step back from your work. Looking at a larger carving from a distance can allow you to see it as others will see it, since your perspective can be impaired while working close to the carving.

Use the photograph to establish where the branches meet the tree canopy. They are not all on the same plane, and you will need to take this into account when working on the underside of the canopy.

Next, start on the trunk, working your way up to the end of the branches. First go over the entire trunk and all branches, roughing them out before going over it again to refine the form. Be careful to give a natural appearance to the tree trunk and branches, including any knots, bumps and twists which would exist in the real thing.

You will need to remove the blank from the cutting board to undercut the trunk slightly and establish its round appearance. Do the same with the branches. Note in many areas the branches are completely undercut and are round in cross-section, especially where they start to meet the canopy.

Be careful when carving the unsupported branches so you don't break them off. If you do break them, use a thick super glue to re-attach the piece before continuing.

COMPLETING CONTOURS

Once the shape is roughed out, the next step is to finish the entire surface. Using the rough surface as a starting point, re-assess the contours and features you want to achieve.

Use lighter, more controlled strokes and begin to refine the detail and smooth out the surfaces, removing as many flat areas and tool marks as possible. Where the tree branches meet the canopy, carefully pare the branch up to the canopy, then cut at the surface of the canopy to remove the waste.

The tree canopy can be left smooth, as shown in the photographs, or you can add some detail to represent leaves. One quick way to accomplish this is to use a power carver with a small burr and roughen up the entire surface of the canopy. Remember though, you may be adding lots of nooks and crannies to collect dust.

Sand the entire carving starting with 150, 180 and finally 220 grit sandpaper but don't sand the canopy if you have roughened it up. Once the sanding is complete, use a tack cloth to remove all sawdust, and finish with several coats of

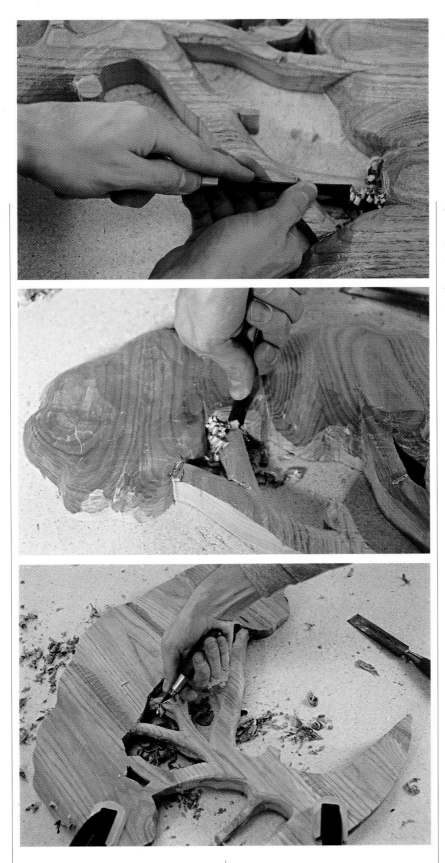

Top left **Paring a branch with a ½in, 13mm No 6 gouge.**
Centre left **Cutting in to define the canopy where the branch meets it.**
Bottom left **Undercutting the branches from the underside of the blank using a carving knife.**
Below **The finished tree mirror.**

show and will hold the mirror flush with the wood.

Two eye hooks are screwed into the tree canopy from behind, next to the mirror clips, and picture wire is attached. The mirror will hang best if you use felt buttons on the mirror clips to hold it evenly out from the wall.

To clean the mirror, remove it from the carving first to avoid breaking the carving and to enable you to clean its entire surface. Lay it on a clean towel or blanket face down, remove the mirror and use your favourite glass cleaner. While you are at it, you can wipe any dust off the carving with a damp cloth. ●

Michel Theriault lives in Ottawa, Canada. His interest in carving started with a hobby knife and a stick. He is self-taught, largely from woodworking magazines and books, and now carves in relief and in the round, specialising in pierced relief mirror frames.

polyurethane, lightly sanding with 220 grit sandpaper in between coats to maintain a smooth finish.

MOUNTING THE MIRROR
The mirror is held onto the tree carving using three metal mirror clips. The two behind the tree canopy are regular clips, the correct size for your mirror thickness, plus a felt pad to prevent scratching the back of the mirror (¼in, 6mm size for ³⁄₁₆in, 5mm thick mirror).

The bottom clip is re-shaped into a U shape with one long side and is screwed into a shallow mortise in the tree carving so the clip will hardly

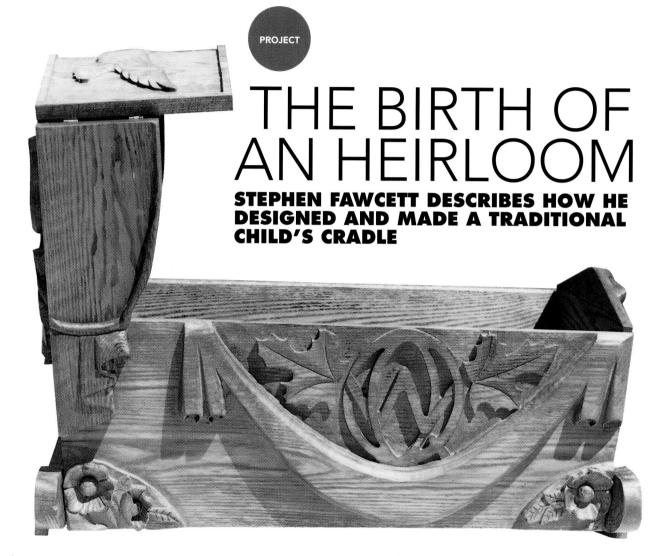

THE BIRTH OF AN HEIRLOOM

STEPHEN FAWCETT DESCRIBES HOW HE DESIGNED AND MADE A TRADITIONAL CHILD'S CRADLE

Above **Side view of the finished cradle.**

I spend most of my professional time as a joiner, so the commission to carve a child's cradle came as a pleasant surprise. I had been doing some joinery work for an elderly Canadian lady living here in England, and she heard that I also do some woodcarving.

Her daughter was expecting her first child over in Alberta, Canada, and as this would be her first grandchild, she wanted to celebrate the occasion by having a traditional wooden cradle made. Since the finished cradle had to be shipped over to Canada and would

be the family heirloom, I decided almost straight away that it had to be a 'flat pack' design.

MADE TO TRAVEL

The brief was that it had to be decorative, functional and portable. A design evolved which allowed the cradle to sit directly on its rockers rather than being suspended. The curvature for the rockers had to be right as there is a relationship with the centre of gravity. Too little curve and the baby would never get to sleep, too much curve and the poor mite would have 'a life on the ocean wave'!

The cradle I designed has solid

sides and ends, and a hood. The hood is hinged and in four pieces which come off separately and fold flat. The end or foot board can be taken off, and the base and sides are all connected and fold flat.

The construction of the base and sides was the most difficult. Because the sides are higher than the base width and are carved in high relief, they had to fold opposite ways, one clockwise, the other anticlockwise. Therefore the two pivots are offset, one higher than the other. The pivots are ¾in, 20mm ramin dowels. The base was let in to each rocker along its whole width, and glued after the carving was finished. This way, the base held the sides and allowed them to swing free.

With all this construction out of the way I could now concentrate on the carving. I used English oak (*Quercus robur*) 2in, 50mm thick boards which had to be edge jointed. Normally I would groove the edges and glue them together using a loose tongue. But because of carving, I could not risk exposing the glued tongue when I cut into the wood, so the boards had to be butt jointed. I put my faith in modern adhesive technology.

I reduced the thickness of the oak by half to get the high relief as shown in the picture of the footboard. I used a router with a ½in, 13mm bit to plough away the bulk, leaving strips of wood standing on which to run the router base. I'm not a purist woodcarver, I will use a knife and fork if I think it will save time and give the desired effect!

Excess material was also left around the outside, about 2in, 50mm to allow the router base to overrun the edges. These were removed later with a large chisel and then finished using a ¾in, 20mm or ½in, 13mm No.12, which is a very shallow gouge, curved or long bent. The ideal tool would have been a macaroni, but my budget will not stretch to such exotic tools. I also used a cabinet scraper to smooth out the background. This method was used to lower the background on all parts of the cradle.

The headboard was also made out of a 2in, 50mm thick oak plank. This was secured by a small piece of timber in the centre extended to form a tenon. The tenon passes through a hole in the base and is then held in place by a turn button screwed to the underside. The sides and ends are held in place with metal plates that interlock. These plates come in mild steel so I had them brass

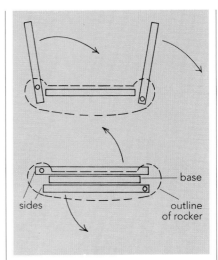

Above **Section through the cradle to show the positioning of the base and sides**
Below **Interlocking plates used to join the sides and ends, brass plated steel**

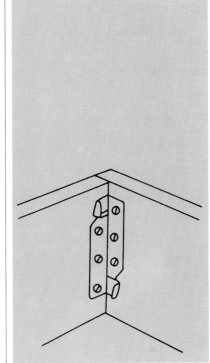

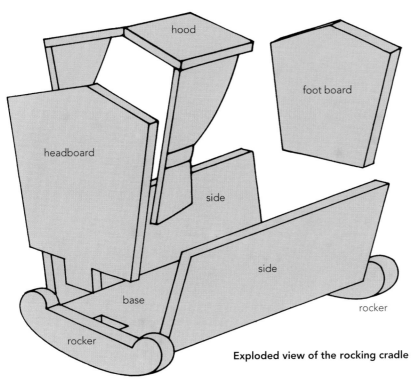

Exploded view of the rocking cradle

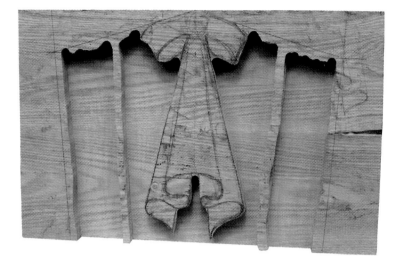

'THE WORKING PROPERTIES OF OAK ARE AFFECTED BY ITS GROWTH'

Above **Work in progress on the footboard of the cradle, ridges have been left to support the router base**
Below **The hood top is decorated with a dove**

plated. Together with the hinges on the hood, these are the only metal parts used on the cradle.

The purpose of the general design was to give the effect of stylised drapery combined with different elements connected with Canada. The flowers on the bottom corners of the sides are dog roses, the emblem of Alberta Province. The position they are in is no accident, these also house the pivots. On each side I have carved maple leaves, the emblem of Canada, and the cyphers of the grandparents, DQ and WQ. The hood was made in four pieces, hinged at the apex and where the top joins the sides, so it all folds flat. The client asked for the hood top to be decorated with a dove, and for the back of the headboard to display the family coat of arms.

TRACING TIPS

I have tried different methods of putting a design from paper to wood, but the best way I have found is to use an overhead projector, the type that are used as teaching aids in schools. The image is drawn onto acetate film, this is then projected directly onto the wood or a sheet of paper which can be moved backwards and forwards to alter the size of the image. The image is then drawn over again with carbon paper underneath, onto the wood.

KNOW YOUR OAK

I have found that the working properties of oak are affected by its growth. If grown quickly it is dense and strong, and hard to work; slowly grown timber is lighter in weight, milder, not as strong and easier to carve. You'd think that it would be the opposite way round! Oak is a slow growing tree, but timber grown on a south facing aspect with good drainage and high rain fall, will produce fast growth. So if you can, choose oak with close annual rings.

The project took me approximately 80 hours labour. The approximate dimensions of the finished cradle are 36 x 24 x 18in, 915 x 610 x 460mm. ●

Left **The headboard, with the family crest**

Stephen Fawcett has been a freelance joiner for seventeen years. He started woodcarving eight years ago and is self-taught, integrating his carving into his joinery work. He is influenced by Art Nouveau, Victorian painting and Science Fiction illustrators and has taught woodworking skills to Y.T.S. students and carving at adult training centres. As a pastime he is building up a collection of figures of historical notoriety such as: Salome, Salambo and Cleopatra.
Stephen Fawcett can be contacted at: 106 Lonsdale Road, Bolton, Gt Manchester, BL1 4PN.
Tel: 01204 847167

BIRD IMPRESSION

ROGER SCHROEDER EXPLAINS HOW HE MADE A MAJESTIC FALCON IN AN IMPRESSIONISTIC STYLE

I am a teacher, woodcarver, cabinet-maker, and an author, although the order of their importance can change on any single day. My full-time job is teaching English, my avocation is writing books and magazine articles, and my hobby is working wood. Sometimes all three areas come together as they did with the carved falcon featured here.

Like many of my teaching colleagues, I wanted to write. Unfortunately, I was not successful authoring the Great American Novel, so I began to write about my hobby: making furniture.

I discovered I could put together technical information in an instructive way. With my early successes at translating wood into words, a publisher asked me to write a book about master North American wildfowl carvers. I had not anticipated, as I began the first of seven birdcarving books, I would be bitten by the carving bug.

Over the years I had watched wildfowl artists grind, saw, burn, insert and paint wood to make wooden birds so realistic they seemed ready to chirp, caw, peep, or quack. I was immediately interested in doing this kind of work, but I was daunted not only by the talent required, but also by the details. I asked myself why I shouldn't use the furniture wood I was familiar with and sculpt much simpler, impressionistic birds from it.

POWERFUL SUBJECT

My first carving was a falcon perched on a craggy rock on a block-shaped base, all carved from a single piece of mahogany (*Swietenia spp*). It was a design concept which I kept over the years, although I later decided the squared base was unnecessary and distracting to the form.

Why falcons? The falcon is noted for its hooked beak, taloned feet, broad, powerful shoulders, and long pointed wings. It also has incredible eyesight. But to me the peregrine, which is what

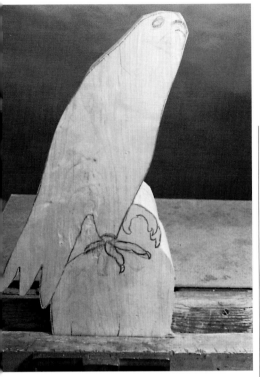

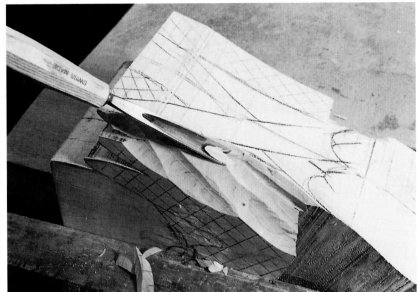

Above **The cutout from a piece of cherrywood, the centre of which ran directly through the middle of the carving.** Below **I drew the outlines of the primary feathers using a draughtsman's triangle that had some flex to it. I relied on a centreline, but wanted the crossing of the primaries to be slightly to its right.**

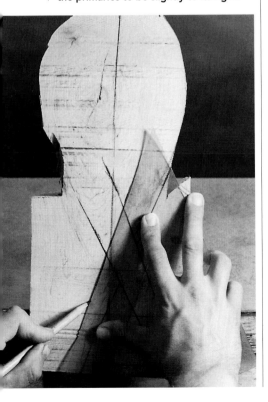

my piece tries to evoke, is the most interesting of all falcons. When it goes into a power dive, it can achieve speeds of up to 200 miles per hour!

But it was not a flying peregrine I wished to carve. Instead, I wanted a bird which had both an active and majestic pose. So I designed one which had its head turned slightly upward. I also elevated one foot above the base.

I may have made the feet even larger than they actually are, but that was because of Rodin. The artist exaggerated the sizes of feet and hands for expressive reasons. It seemed a good idea since I was doing an interpretive wood sculpture, instead of a feather perfect bird. I chose rugged rock for it to stand on, which is typical of a peregrine's habitat.

I had a log of black cherrywood (*Prunus serotina*) that had had some time to season. I like the look of this wood because while it has a richness to the colour that gets darker with age, it does not have a showy and distracting grain.

It can be risky business, however, working with large pieces of cherry because rotten spots can show up after you are well into the carving. On the plus side, the tight grain gives a highly polished look. So I took my chances with the available log.

ROUGH CUTS

I spent a lot of time with the patterns, both side and front profiles. By doing this a lot of problems can be worked

Wood that could not be removed with the bandsaw had to be taken out with handtools. Here I used a no.14 12mm, ½in V-parting tool to outline the areas that would be intact. A large, flat gouge got rid of the excess wood.

out beforehand. The patterns I made are full size: the peregrine on its base is 16in, 405mm tall.

I don't like working with a rough log but prefer to work with a squared-up piece on which I can lay out my patterns. After squaring the log, I cut away the waste wood for one profile, tack-glue that wood back in place, and cut out the other profile. What is left is a cubist form that I imagine Picasso would have been proud of.

The crossed primaries in this kind of bird sculpture were particularly challenging. Many of the realistic bird artists do insertions, but that does not work well with interpretive sculpture. Also, because of the position of these feathers, it was not possible to remove much wood with the bandsaw. A lot of wood had to be taken away by hand.

I began by laying out the crossed primaries with a flexible draughtsman's triangle and blocked out the wood around them which had to be removed. The best tool I found for outlining is a large V-parting tool. This was followed by a wide gouge that had a deep sweep. At this point I tried to get rid of as much wood as possible.

Many of the tools I use are Swiss-

The primaries project out of the rear of the bird, so both body and feathers have to flow together. I spent a lot of time shaping the crossed primaries. Here I worked with a no.3 35mm, 1⅜in fishtail gouge.

I used the flexible shaft grinding tool and a rotary carbide rasp to round off the carving marks and smooth the surface.

Above The falcon's left foot is lifted and forward of its right foot. I used a no.8 25mm, 1in gouge to remove wood. Below To take away wood from between the feet and from under the belly, I used a 25mm, 1in diameter Forstner bit in a drill. I used a sighting line to help establish the angle.

made. Most carvers who use these tools agree the steel is hard and keeps an edge. The tools also have comfortable handles, and their octagonal shapes prevent them from rolling around on the bench. They are expensive in the United States, but well worth the investment.

I spent a great deal of time on the primaries because they had to be undercut and overlap. To add to this challenge, they were not flat but slightly convex. I also had to keep them rather on the heavy side so they would not be fragile. This meant I had to create the illusion of thinness while in fact keeping them quite thick.

BODY SHAPING

The next step was rounding the body. I started at the rear of the bird where the primaries entered the wings and worked my way around toward the front. For this I used a large fishtail gouge with a shallow sweep.

As with the area around the primaries I wanted to get rid of wood as quickly as I could. Before I rounded

the front, however, I stopped to define the wings, using a small V-parting tool. The bird had started to get some shape.

I'm a firm believer in using power tools for this kind of carving wherever possible. One I found most useful was the flexible shaft grinder with an adjustable speed control box.

Combined with an elongated rotary carbide rasp, I did a lot of shaping and smoothing on the surface of the wood to get rid of the carving marks. I was careful, however, to work from both sides of a centreline which I applied with pencil.

PROBLEM SOLVING

I knew the feet would give me problems. The bird's left foot was not only lifted, but well in front of the right foot. This meant relieving the left foot by taking away wood to its right.

But the problems did not stop there. The bird's belly was also elevated above the base, so I had to take out wood from between the rump, tail and base as well as between the two legs. This looked like a carver's nightmare.

The solution I came up with was to drill out as much wood as possible.

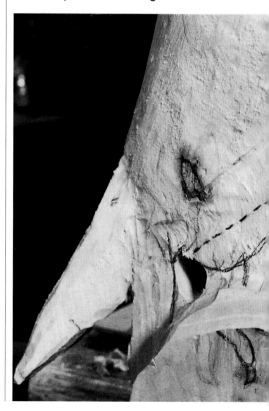

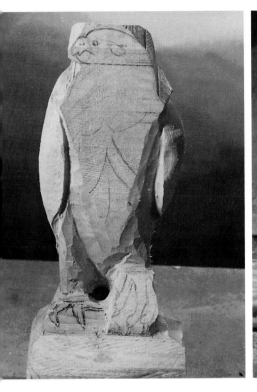

Above **Front view of the body in progress.**
Above right **Here I outlined the foot using a no.11 5mm, ⅜in veiner.**
Below right **I used the no.8 25mm, 1in gouge to shape the neck.**

What made this possible was the use of a Forstner bit. I suppose I could have used other bits, but the Forstner does not seem to wander or do much damage to the walls of the hole. I used it and I was successful with it. I was able to carve away the rest of the wood with small gouges. Once I had the feet

roughly defined, I moved on, rounding and shaping the belly area.

Some problems were solved but others kept cropping up. What to do with the toes? Though it seemed like a good idea to keep the foot off the base, I knew it would have a lot of end grain exposed, making the toes very fragile. Yet I wanted as much wood removed as I could between and behind them. I decided to use a small Forstner bit to drill out wood behind the toes, while keeping them attached to the rocky base.

THE HEAD

I needed to take a break from the lower body and feet and went to work on the head. First, I made sure a centreline went up through the head. Then I drew in another line which indicated

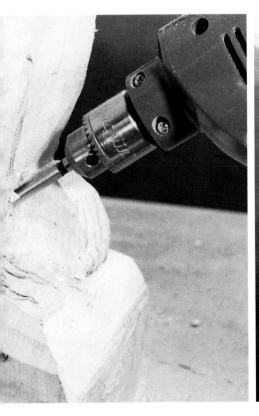

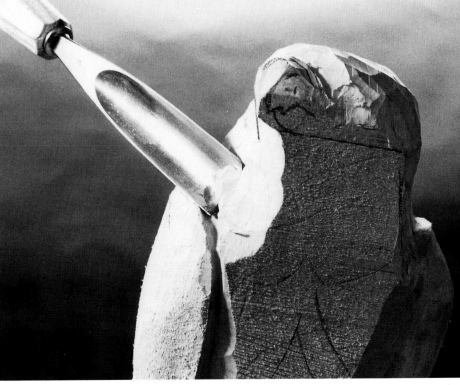

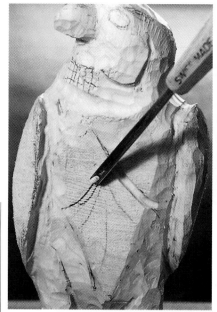 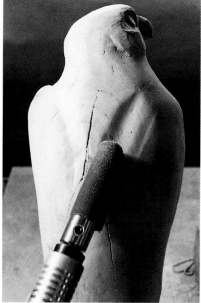 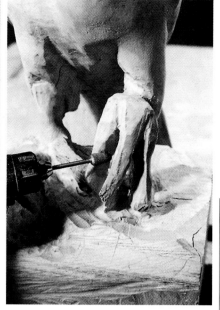

Left **I defined the breast bones using the no.11 5mm, ³⁄₁₆in veiner.**
Centre **I wanted to give some definition to the area between the middle of the back and the scapular feathers. After removing wood with gouges, I softened the area using a cushioned sanding drum.**
Right **A file cutter was useful for shaping the toes of the raised foot.**

how the head was to be turned.

Next I shaped the head, which was where the real fun and challenge began. I ended up not only turning the head, but also tilting it some 20°! While doing that, I had to be sure the head still had a smooth flow into the shoulder area.

After I rounded the head I had to remove wood from the area of the beak. This caused some consternation because proportions were critical. I did not want my bird looking like a caricature. Instead, I wanted a realistic beak as a focal point. I shaped the top of it, but kept the underside heavy where the mandibles met. The final detailing I saved for last.

It was back to the feet and how to take wood from between the toes. I returned to power tools, but replaced the flexible shaft grinder with a Dremel Moto-Tool. This and a needle-shaped rotary carbide rasp removed wood as quickly as a dentist drills out a tooth.

DEFINITION

A lot more definition work had to be done on the body, especially on the feathers surrounding the raised foot and the flanks of the bird flowing into primaries. The primaries themselves

had to be thinned down and given more definition where they crossed.

Refine, refine, refine. That was the process for the next several days, as I worked each area into the next, taking away more wood with small gouges and giving greater definition to those tricky toes.

It was at this point I took some liberties with the chest of the bird. I wanted to give it a muscular, chesty look, which would not really be seen on the live bird. This is what one well-known carver called giving the bird 'muscles and bumps'.

To do this, I used a small V-parting tool and carved an inverted V on the upper chest. I then removed wood below the V and the result was a strong and muscular bird. Not only that, it broke up what would have been a broad, flat surface which I think would have taken away from the overall look.

I also wanted to break up the flatness of the back. I defined the bases of the wings with shallow V cuts, making a V shape that extended from the shoulders down. With a shallow gouge I removed wood from either side of the grooves, and used a ¾in, 20mm diameter cushioned drum sander to soften the depression and actually flatten it out so that it would be more subtle.

When it came to the rocks, I knew I wanted something that was almost abstract, that had deep cracks, and would not take away from the falcon. I cut V grooves and widened those with other gouges. What I ended up with were vertical fissures and irregular planes.

EYES AND BEAK

When I was near completion, I went back to the head to work on the eyes and finish the beak. A very useful tool for removing wood from around the eyes was a small fishtail gouge.

To shape the beak, I found myself putting aside the gouges and using power bits that ranged from serrated cutters called stump cutters to ruby carvers, so-called because of the mineral grit bonded to the bit's surface.

Then I sanded the body using sanding rolls and sanding drums. Areas I couldn't get at with these accessories I sanded by hand, using papers that went up to 220 grit.

To finish the peregrine I used a Deft semi-gloss brushing lacquer which is durable and dries quickly. The best compliments I received on the piece have been several blue ribbons. ●

Roger Schroeder is a prolific writer and lecturer on woodworking, construction, sculpture and carving, as well as a cabinetmaker and amateur carver. He combines these activities with a full-time job as a high school English teacher, specialising in teaching creative writing and research.

BANDSAW BASICS

JEREMY WILLIAMS GIVES SOME USEFUL TIPS ON WHAT CARVERS SHOULD LOOK FOR WHEN CHOOSING A BANDSAW

This article on bandsaws is not a 'best buy' kind of survey, because these days there are a number of really good machines on the market, and in the final analysis selection will be largely a matter of personal preference.

But even with such a wide choice of good equipment available, it does not mean you should buy blind. There are various points you need to check out before parting with your money, and it will prove useful to have some prior knowledge.

I hope I have covered most, if not all, you need to know. Even so, the wise prospective buyer will doubtless wish to glean further knowledge from fellow woodworkers, and to question suppliers at stores and woodworking exhibitions.

If possible put any model that appeals to a practical test. Do not be content to watch an expert zinging wood through a demonstration machine with practised ease.

Where a proprietary name of make has been used in this article it is to illustrate a particular feature, or because that photograph was sourced from that manufacturer or supplier. It is not necessarily that I wish to promote that make.

Buying a bandsaw is not something to be rushed. After you have bought some carving tools and set up a work-station, it could be the next important thing. More and more, carvers are turning to power tools to do much of the tedious roughing out work. In the case of large scale work much is now done with chainsaws.

While some people still believe you must use only hand tools, it can be darned hard graft, and mechanical aids do make sense. Novice carvers, especially, can get a mental block when faced with an irregular piece of wood.

They invariably find it easier to visualise the three-dimensional shape when the wood has been sawn to show something of the basic form.

For general work, both sculpture and relief, a bandsaw can prove invaluable. It will cut the profile, plan view and frontal outline shapes of patterns. Once you have one you will wonder how you ever got by without it!

Manufacturers have to cater for the diverse needs of the whole spectrum of woodworkers, from the requirements of the small scale model maker to the needs of skilled cabinet makers, and from those who hack wood for fun, or for profit as well as for pleasure, to what the really dedicated woodcarver who works full-time wants. So there is a wide range of bandsaws offered.

Some are small, relatively inexpensive, and unable to cope with all but thin timber. Then there are medium capacity ones to suit most amateurs' needs, and there are the ones which have considerable capacity.

The danger is to buy purely on price and to go for low cost without regard to the essential features needed for the particular type of work the saw will have to do. Deficiencies will only become all too apparent once you have got the kit unpacked, set up and working. And then it will be too late.

What are the main pointers we need to be concerned with when planning to buy a suitable piece of kit? Here's my check list with explanations:

THREE WHEEL BANDSAWS

Lower priced bandsaws are invariably of small depth cutting capacity, though the width of entry (the throat) offered by most may be good. More often than not they have a triangular, three-wheel configuration (see drawing).

Metal fatigue causes blades to break. With three wheels the bandsaw blade is subjected to a lot of flexing, more than on two-wheel models. This will quickly induce metal fatigue. Hence it is not uncommon for blades to break at frequent intervals on three-wheel bandsaws, and this can prove costly.

A three-wheel drive means more blade flexing.

The other drawing illustrates the passage of the blade on a two-wheel system. Note the wheels themselves are of a reasonably large diameter, about 255mm, 10in or more. The actual size depends on the size and capacity of the bandsaw itself. This means the blade has far less flexing to do than on the three-wheel models, and consequently there is less induced metal fatigue.

Tip: Check the number of wheels and their diameter before you buy.

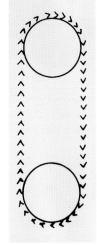

Above **Two wheels means less flexing so blades last longer. The wheels are also larger.**

CUTTING CAPACITY

Three-wheel saws usually have only moderate depth cutting capacity. While this may not be a problem for anyone doing miniature work, and clearly there are people who need only this type of saw, it could certainly present difficulties if you make average size carvings using blocks of wood about house brick size or larger.

Whereas most three-wheel types have a cutting depth of only about 75mm, 3in, the two-wheelers will cut much thicker material. But three-wheel saws invariably have good capacity throats, some have really wide entries, which makes them able to accommodate wide boards.

A Rexon three-wheel bandsaw from Axminster (APTC). This one incorporates a disc sander.

Anyone who specialises in relief carvings, and who may need the wide lateral entry rather than great depth of cut, could find a small three-wheeler sufficient. Otherwise opt for a two-wheel type.

Tip: Make certain the bandsaw has the capacity you need.

TWO-WHEEL TYPES

The majority of carvers need at some stage to cut thick timber. The run-of-the-mill two-wheel saws are undoubtedly the ones to consider, and there is certainly a wide choice on the market. Ideally you should

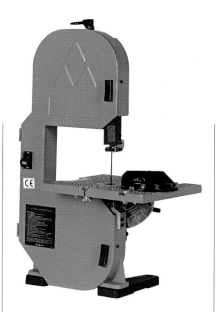

Above **A Delta two-wheel bandsaw from APTC.**
Below **The APTC Model BS350 with the door open to show the wheels.**

look for a saw with not less than 150mm, 6in depth of cut, and one which can cut wood 200mm, 8in thick is preferable. Go for a throat entry not under 305mm, 12in wide.
Tip: Extra capacity is a wise investment.

Above **Axminster (APTC) Model BS350 two-wheel bandsaw.**

TILTING TABLE

The table of a good and well made bandsaw will be precision cast and machined, usually of aluminium. More expensive makes, such as the highly regarded Startrite range have ground steel or cast iron tables.

The table itself should have the facility to be tilted from horizontal to an angle of 45°. This can prove a boon, though one which may not be used too often. For example, it is useful if for whatever reason more wood has to remain on one part of an outline shape than on other parts. Also, you can angle cut, as when sawing a plinth to shape.

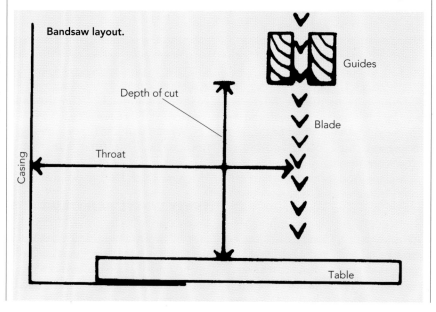

Bandsaw layout.

One of the Startrite range.

TABLE ACCESSORIES

Most tables are able to accept accessories, such as a rip fence, used as a guide when sawing, or a mitre fence for cutting angles. Some makes have a circle cutting attachment, which while of primary interest to turners for cutting bowl blanks can be of use to a carver wishing to make round mirrors, for example.

Tip: Some accessories are worth having.

RIP FENCES

Some manufacturers at exhibitions, as many readers are sure to know, demonstrate how well their product can cut wafer thin veneers from, say, 100mm, 4in thick stock held against a rip fence. This is usually done with a wide blade. But narrow blades can be prone to wander along the path of least resistance through the grain when rip cutting. Much depends on how carefully the setting up adjustments have been carried out in the first place, and how good the blade itself is.

When wandering happens with a rip fence in place, the blade itself can be bent by an excess of pressure being brought to bear between it and the fence. This especially occurs when cutting thick blocks.

Tip: Sometimes you may not wish to cut using a rip fence, but it is still worth having.

MOTORS

The majority of bandsaws on the market use motors of between 0.5 and 0.75hp and are adequate for amateur requirements. Most drive the lower wheel, in a two-wheel system, via a V-belt and stepped pulley to give two operating speeds at around 300 and 800/1000rpm.

Some large capacity machines use direct drive motors, which tend to be more expensive, but to off-set this there is the advantage of little or no loss of power, nor a belt to slip. Direct drive motors can be switched electrically to low/high speeds, and some even offer a selection of three speeds.

But for most people's needs the normal belt drive is sufficient and offers trouble-free operation. For example, my own De Walt bandsaw (now marketed under the Elu name) must be all of 20 years old. It has worked hard all its life, but the belt is the original and hasn't stretched at all.

The drive wheels that power the loop of blade need to be rubber coated, and ideally there should be a small cleaning brush fitted to sweep the lower wheel free of dust, which otherwise could cause the blade to slip. The higher priced saws have dynamically balanced wheels for vibration-free running.

Tip: Don't scrimp on the motor.

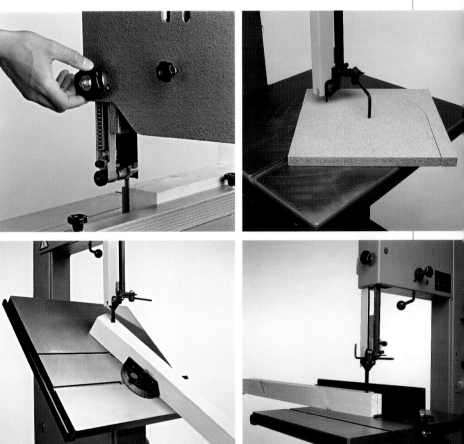

Top **Elu cutting depth guide.**
Above **Startrite tilting table.**

Top **Startrite circle cutting attachment.**
Above **Startrite rip fence in use.**

CONSTRUCTION

Just as you should avoid buying too small, do not buy a bandsaw which is cheaply made, or one where the major parts are of plastic. The stresses and strains on the main frame are considerable when the blade is under tension.

By the way, it is not a good idea to try and make your own. I was once introduced to a home-made job by its enthusiastic owner, who had constructed it from offcuts of 50 x 50mm, 2 x 2in and bits of ply. With a flourish he switched it on for the very first time . . . and it just fell apart with much whizzing and screeching!
Tip: Make sure the model has a good, strong frame.

BLADE ADJUSTMENTS

On most popular models you will find a knob on top of the frame, which when turned moves the upper wheel vertically. This increases/decreases blade tension. Blades should never be over-tight, nor too slack.

Elu 3401 showing blade tensioning knob on top.

Guides and thrust wheel.

Some makes incorporate an indicator to show the degree of pressure and how tensioned the blade is. For those that do not, a fair guess is when you can flex the blade from side to side by about 13mm, ½in but no more. You should never have the blade over-tight.

At the rear of the bandsaw there should be a further control knob which connects with the axle of the upper wheel. This provides fore and aft adjustment so the blade can be made to run truly vertically. If the blade is out of alignment, sooner or later it will work itself to the edge of one of the wheels and come off.

But no matter how well the blade is set up and correctly tensioned, it will invariably run off the drive wheels if you try and reverse out of a cut while the blade is still in motion.
Tip: Precise adjustment controls are needed for correct blade alignment.

SAFETY

Of all the power equipment used in woodwork, the bandsaw is one of the safest, provided it is used sensibly.

The on/off switch should be mounted on the front and be fully accessible when the machine is in use. You need to be able to get to it quickly in an emergency. The switch needs to be of the type that has to be re-set after power failure, and its casing should prevent ingress of wood dust.

Current safety regulations require the cabinet door or main cover box to be fitted with a microswitch to prevent operation with the blade exposed.

Another safety feature is how much time it takes for the blade to come to rest when you press the stop button. Many makers seem coy to quote an actual time delay figure, which I feel is a pity, although most state their product conforms to EU safety requirements. This I gather is less than 10 seconds, which is what Startrite quote in their literature.

Safety features have certainly advanced in recent years. There is an ancient bandsaw still in daily use not far from where I live which literally has a stopping time calculated in minutes, not seconds. Imagine the effect that could have.

The outer casing should contain a dust extraction port.
Tip: Check for safety features.

BLADE GUIDES

The guides which control the position of the blade lie at the very heart of any bandsaw. Not only do they need to be adequate for the job they have to do, but they need to be easy to adjust, as adjustments have to be made every time a blade is changed to a new one, or to one of a different width, and in some cases to take up guide wear.

Those saws which have either capped Allen screws, or use a lever

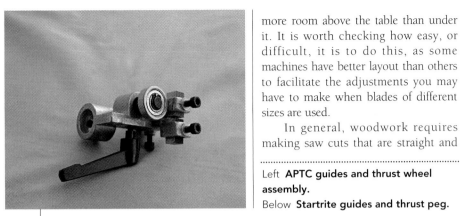

Left **APTC guides and thrust wheel assembly.**
Below **Startrite guides and thrust peg.**

more room above the table than under it. It is worth checking how easy, or difficult, it is to do this, as some machines have better layout than others to facilitate the adjustments you may have to make when blades of different sizes are used.

In general, woodwork requires making saw cuts that are straight and true, and sometimes these cuts are long. To do this it is usual to employ a fairly wide blade, 12mm, ½in or even wider. But the cutting of carving blanks is invariably a very different matter, as there can be many twists and turns to cope with, and it is all too easy to burn the wood if the blade is too big.

To overcome this, and to cope with the tight shapes, a narrow contour blade, say 4.5mm, ³⁄₁₆in is normally used. But these small width blades can quickly wear out the part of a static guide they touch as they twist and flex.

Up to a few years ago you got only plastic or metal fixed, or static, guides fitted to medium price range bandsaws. And one make used wood blocks, not such a bad idea at that, as you could easily and cheaply make your own from scrap hardwood.

While you may still find these old type solid metal guides being used on some machines, others have changed to roller-bearing guides, now used for example on the Kity 613, or use lubricated cool blocks. These work well with narrow blades, for although there may be wear, it matters not if the blade itself gets embedded into the wall of the block as it twists and turns, it still works.

Tip: Check what type of guides are used.

STANDS

Large bandsaws may come with in-built stands, but the ones the average hobby carver would tend to use seldom do. Their stands are extra, and in one or two cases they can be costly, though others make only a reasonable charge.

But a stand is not particularly difficult to construct, and will last for years as long as it is robustly made in the first place. Some bandsaws can be table top mounted.

Tip: Budget for the cost of a stand.

Several manufacturers supplied photographs and technical information for this article, and I am also grateful to Ian Styles at Axminster Power Tool Centre for his co-operation.

Finally, some makes to consider and, as a guideline, their recommended retail prices including VAT:

Axminster Power Tools APTC:
BS350CE £439.95
Elu EBS 3401 £512.30
Delta 28-190 £533
Inca Euro 260 £599.25
Kity 613 £611
Kity 413 £439
Startrite 301S £667.40

Tip: Shop around for a good deal. ●

For further details contact:

**Axminster Power Tool Centre,
Chard Street, Axminster,
Devon EX13 5DZ.
Tel: 01297 33656.**

**Elu Power Tools (De Walt),
Tel: 01242 545345.**

**Delta UK,
Westwings House,
Station Road, Guiseley ,
W. Yorkshire LS20 8BX.
Tel: 01943 873535.**

**Inca (Tyme Machines),
Paragon House, Flex Meadows,
The Pinnacles, Harlow,
Essex CM19 5TJ.
Tel: 01279 418336.**

**Kity (Stayer Group),
61 High Street, Chobham,
Surrey GU24 8AF.
Tel: 01276 856985.**

**Startrite Machine Tool Co,
Norman Close, Rochester,
Kent ME2 7JU.
Tel: 01634 298200.**

locking arrangement, are the easiest to adjust. Spanners invariably seem more fiddly, especially when they have to be used underneath the saw table.

Guides are mounted in pairs on either side of the blade, above and below the table, to keep the blade running true, and to prevent it shifting from side to side when cutting. Thrust wheels, sometimes called thrust bearings or roller bearings, are fitted as well, above and below the table, at the back of the blade to stop it moving backwards when cutting pressure is applied. If it were to move too far backwards the teeth would ruin the blade guides.

These thrust wheels form part of the blade guide assembly. They are used by all but one maker, who on a particular bandsaw employs a hardened steel peg instead.

It is not unusual to find it easier to adjust the upper guides and thrust wheel than the lower set, as there is

DANCING DOBBIN

GEOFF BRADLEY TELLS HOW HE MADE A HOBBYHORSE FOR THE STAFFORD MORRISMEN

Stafford Morrismen prepare to dance with the Hobbyhorse

One festive dinner, early in the New Year, I was asked by friends who are Morris Dancers if I would carve a horse's head which they could use to make a Hobbyhorse. This is an ancient tradition which you can see depicted in an old enamelled window, now held in the Victoria and Albert Museum in London.

The general requirements were for a realistic head, about two thirds life size, light in weight with a mouth capable of collecting money at events, and strong enough to be attached to a metal frame around the dancer's body.

To make it sufficiently light, and possible to insert a mechanism for collecting money, I decided to use a hollow, built-up construction. Cedar

(*Cedrus spp*) was the ideal wood and I had some boards which had been stripped from the front of a house. These were planed up for me into boards 2¾ x ½ x 24in, 70 x 13 x 610mm. I needed 28 of these boards.

I gave a lot of thought to how the mouth should be designed to collect money. I rejected the idea of a hinged jaw as being ugly, deciding that the head would be carved with the mouth open, and the tongue would be designed to take the money, then flick it back down the throat.

I agreed with the Morrismen that the eyes should be carved and the mane would be made of real horsehair. The length of the head was to be 16in, 405mm and the neck 20in, 510mm. The angle of the neck to the head would be 112.5°, this being one of the set angles on my Nobex mitre saw.

HORSE DRAWINGS

It is fairly easy to obtain front and side views of a horse's head from books, or by photographing or drawing a live animal. Although the open mouth had to be adjusted to suit the needs of the design, the most difficult design feature was to work out the cross sections and calculate the dimensions of the built-up box sections.

I obtained the necessary cross sections from the excellent book by Ellenberger, Baim and Dittrick *Atlas of Animal Anatomy for Artists*. This enabled me to plan the size of the box sections and the amount of additional wood which had to be laminated onto the appropriate parts.

I prepared a cutting list and built

Below **Head box section with top detached**
Below right **Section A–A through the head**

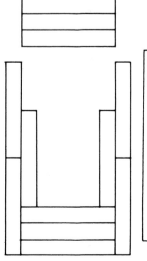
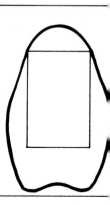

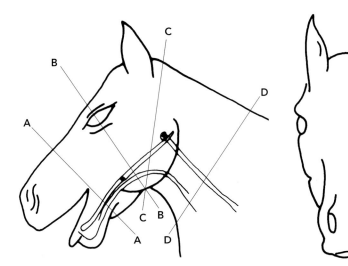

Above **Side view showing the tongue, spring and cord**
Right **Front view**

up the head and neck as two separate boxes without fixing the tops. I used Evostick Waterproof Wood Adhesive to laminate the boards and wooden dowels provided extra strength, holding the sides to the bottoms.

I took care to have the grain all running in the same direction, and as far as possible to put the same coloured wood together. When the boards were cleaned up, a wide variation in the colour of the wood was revealed, ranging from dark brown to light orange.

I then fixed the head box to the neck box with adhesive and dowels, adding strength to this joint by overlapping the side neck boards with the side head boards.

At a later stage in the carving, where the dowels were showing, I drilled them out to a depth of ½in, 13mm and inserted cedar wood plugs. The top lid of the head box, which was three boards thick, and the top lid of the neck box, which was five boards thick, were both left unfixed at this stage to create an L-shaped, open topped box.

INITIAL SHAPING

I cut the mouth and roughly shaped the mouth and jaw so that the tongue

Below **Section B–B with extra pieces laminated to the head box**

Below **Section C–C**
Right **Section D–D through the neck box**

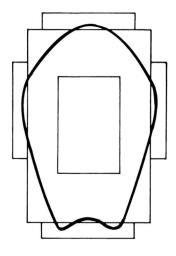

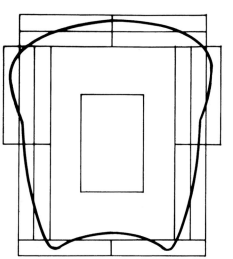

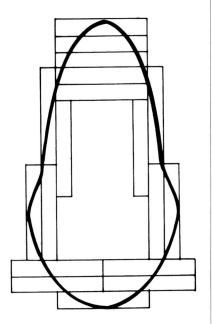

overall carving could be carried out. The cedar wood proved very difficult to cut cleanly with gouges, so much of the shaping was carried out with a coping saw, flat and rounded Stanley surforms, and a half round rasp.

The ears were made by laminating the cedar boards to make rectangular blocks which I let into the head before shaping them on the outside with the surform and rasp, and on the inside with a spoon gouge. The final detailed carving and shaping included eyes, nostrils, ears and neck muscles.

As with all carving I needed continually to look very carefully at live horses, as well as at numerous photographs and drawings. My experience is that customers often find a carving more acceptable if some of its notable features are accentuated. On the horse's head, these were the nostrils and the neck muscles.

FINISHING

I finished the whole head with a fine riffler, followed by sanding with medium and fine garnet paper. I cut a groove down the back of the neck for the mane to be fitted later. I glued and screwed a 1½in, 38mm thick block of ash to fill the bottom end of the neck, leaving a small space at the bottom for the money to fall out. This block was to provide the anchorage to the metal frame.

It was only at this stage that I fixed the shaped lid of the neck box with two screws, in such a way that the screw heads would be hidden by the mane, but could be removed if necessary to get at the tongue mechanism.

The different coloured cedar wood boards meant the carving had to be stained to a consistent colour. I used Liberon's walnut spirit wood dye, but this gave an effect which I felt was too dull and dark, so I lightened it with Liberon's wood bleacher, then re-stained with Liberon yew spirit wood dye. This produced a very acceptable chestnut colour, with some pleasing variations.

I sealed the model with two coats of Ronseal mattcoat clear varnish. The first coat I brushed on and lightly sanded, the second I brushed on and wiped off immediately with a cloth. For the final polish I used a homemade mixture of pure turpentine, carnauba and beeswax followed by a coat of Liberon's Black Bison wax polish.

HORSEHAIR MANE

I bought a white mane of real horsehair attached to a strip of hide from the Rocking Horse Shop, York. This had to be soaked overnight to make it pliable before being butted up to and nailed along the groove which I had made down the neck. I cut a separate piece of mane and fixed it to form the forelock. The horse's head was now ready to be handed over to the Morrismen to make their Hobbyhorse.

Bob Jenkins, one of the Stafford Morrismen, made the leather bridle and the metal body frame was made by another Morrisman – Jeff Miller. The skirt and shoulder straps were made by his wife Petula.

Just under six months after the first discussion on the project, the Hobbyhorse made its first public appearance at Tideswell Wakes, Derbyshire, where it danced with the Stafford Morrismen in their torchlight procession and other dances. It has since appeared at the Abbots Bromley Horn Dance Festival and is a popular feature at the Stafford Morrismen's events. ●

Top **General shaping to the head and neck prior to the ears being fitted**
Above **Geoff Bradley completing the carving**

mechanism could be fitted. The tongue was shaped from laminated plywood, which after being painted matt red was riveted to a clock spring 20mm, ¾in wide. This in turn I screwed to the inside of the throat which I had rounded to a curve up to the front of the mouth.

I attached a nylon cord to the back of the tongue and took it round a spindle inserted at the bottom of the neck, so a tug of the cord gave a flick of the tongue to send any money collected down the neck.

I next glued the lid of the head box in place, and held the lid of the neck box in place with a clamp so the

Geoff Bradley is a retired librarian who took up woodcarving as a hobby in 1970. He was taught by Wilf Burt and Dennis Parsons, from whom he gained much inspiration. Geoff carves both three dimensional and relief work, furniture and models of animals and birds. His work has found its way to France, Italy and Denmark as well as this country. He undertakes carving commissions for David Hanlon at Designs in Wood, Amerton Farm, Near Stafford. He is also a member of the British Woodcarvers Association.

HORSE PLAY

REG PARSONS DESCRIBES HOW TO CARVE A PAIR OF FIGHTING HORSES

The horse is an elegantly beautiful and spirited creature which has featured in paintings, sculpture and literature more than any other great mammal. Since first painted in the caves of early man, its beauty and spirit has captured men's hearts and minds and become the stuff of dreams and legends.

One of the major problems in carving a horse in wood is the vulnerability of the slender legs to damage. I have partly overcome this by using Cornish elm (*Ulmus stricta*) which is a particularly tough and sinewy wood. I have arranged the grain so it runs vertically up the legs for strength.

The forelegs of horse A, which will inevitably be cross-grained whichever way the grain is arranged, are left firmly connected to the other horse. This means one horse supports the other, and I have also arranged for both tails to be supported throughout their

Side view of the finished fighting horses

....

length. Horse tail A is supported by the extended right rear leg, and the tail of horse B is supported by the flank.

Elm also has the advantage of being well figured, and the grain is not too obtrusive with a lovely rich brown colouring. English elm (*Ulmus procera*) would be just as suitable, with its slightly less wild grain and its lighter colouring. The points I have made on strength should be carefully considered if you deviate from the design in any way.

The sweeps of the gouges mentioned here are those I used in the carving, but similar available sweeps would probably be suitable.

First obtain the wood and examine it closely for shakes or knots which will have to be avoided, or areas of grain or figure which can be incorporated in the design.

Next produce a template from the side view drawing given here, scaling it up to fit the available wood. Remember to leave a block around the heads, as indicated by the dotted lines, to enable them to be turned to an angle later.

WORKHOLDER

It is important at this point to consider how you will hold the work securely in the vice as the work proceeds. If you do not have a universal joint, the simplest and cheapest solution is to firmly screw a T shaped hardwood block 3 x 3 x 5in, 75 x 75 x 125mm to the bottom of the base, using the arms of the T to take the screws.

This will enable the work to be rotated in 90° stages, and where necessary tilted over to get at the more inaccessible areas. Alternatively, you could construct a hardwood universal joint for use with a 4in, 100mm engineer's vice, as described in my book *Woodcarving: a Manual of Techniques*.

BLOCKING IN

With the wood now securely held, use the template to clearly and accurately mark out the side view on the block and then remove wood from outside of the lines with a bandsaw.

Alternatively, you can saw in radially at close intervals across the grain and then split the wood away between the cuts with a large bosting in gouge such as a ⅝in, 15mm No.7. Then clear up the ragged surface left with a round surform.

The wood between the two horses and between the legs of horse B can be removed with a jigsaw after first drilling in a hole vertically to take the blade. Most jigsaw blades cut to a depth of about 2⅝in, 65mm so even a 5in, 125mm wide block can be cut out if the block is approached from each side. Take care to leave a generous margin for error as the jigsaw blade is easily tilted over at an angle when cutting to that sort of depth.

Remove the unwanted wood around the legs down to about a quarter of the way into the block and then mark on the rear view of the tails ensuring the tail of horse A is firmly connected to the right rear leg. Remove wood from outside of the lines ensuring the tail of horse B is well defined where it crosses the horse's flank and the forelegs of horse A are also clearly defined.

Draw on the rear views, noting both horses' heads are not only turned but also tilted over. It is extremely important to make a generous allowance where both heads touch so the area can be refined later.

Remove wood from outside of the lines, noting in particular all surfaces should be kept flat at this stage, with no attempt to round over or shape the work until you start bosting in. Also, you should not remove wood from between the legs, when viewed from the front or rear, until much later when the external shape has been accurately established. This also applies to the ears.

Prepare templates of both heads and use them to mark out each side of the head blocks, remove wood from outside of the lines and define the ears at the same time.

Once the external shape of the legs is absolutely accurate, wood can be removed from between them. Even now you should leave them a little on the thick side to refine them later when you have carved in the muscle and bone.

BOSTING IN

At this stage the carving is shaped and begins to come to life. You must obtain and study photographs and pictures of

Below Horses are blocked in, legs and tails are defined

Below Blocked out rear view of horse A before bosting in

Far left **Wood is removed from outside the lines, keeping all surfaces flat until bosting in commences**

Left **The ears are defined**

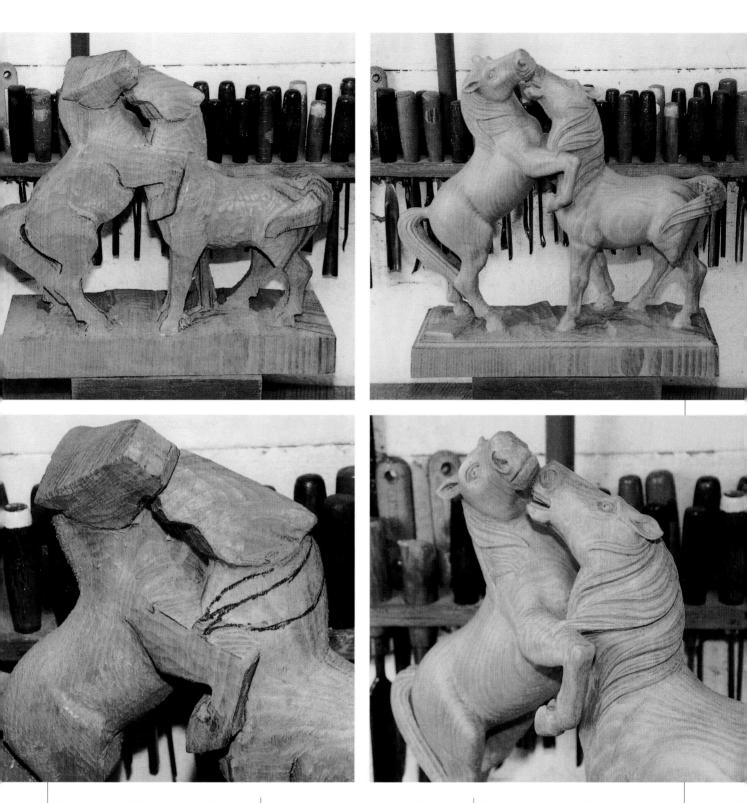

Top and above **The bodies are shaped, leaving a generous amount of wood on the necks**

horses throughout the rest of the carving if a realistic and interesting carving is to be achieved. I cannot emphasise this point enough.

First shape both bodies as pictured, leaving a generous amount of wood on the necks for the manes to be carved on later. The forelegs of horse A should be left until the width of the body has been accurately established.

Note the right foreleg of horse A throws out to the right for greater realism. Once the bodies have been bosted in, the heads and legs can be shaped and related in a natural way to the bodies.

THE HEADS

This area is the most difficult part of the carving, and you should take great care over it. It is easier to relate one head naturally to the other one if one

Top and above **Note the centre depression on the ears is shallow and comes to a point at the bottom. A small tendril of hair flows across the cheek of horse B**

of the heads is almost completed before you start on the second.

The ears – Both ears are laid right back with only the tips being freed from the head. Horses' ears are a particularly subtle and beautiful shape, and they have a marked effect upon the appearance of the whole head. The centre depression is shallow and comes to a point at the bottom.

Eyes and nostrils – An excited fighting horse's eyes would be dilated, so most of the eyeball would be visible. To form the eyeball, stab vertically down with a gouge which has a sweep fitting the required curvature, such as a ¼in, 6mm No.9.

Then rotate the gouge to partly complete the circle leaving about 10° at the top where it is covered by the eyelid.

The eyeball can then be rounded over either with a small, flattish gouge such as a ⅛in, 3mm No.3 or a sharp craft knife. Use the knife to cut a triangle in the front and back corners of the eyeball and form a channel right round the eye with a ⅛in, 3mm No.10. Finally, make a small hole in the centre of the eyeball to bring it to life, being careful not to split the eyeball.

The nostrils are situated right at the end of the muzzle. The tendency here is to carve them in a little way back. The centre depression is formed with a ⅛in, 3mm No.10, preferably using a veiner to get down to the required depth. Take great care not to crumble the nostril edges. Then form a depression round the exterior of the nostril to give a flared effect. The flaring needs to be pronounced in this carving.

Mouth – The mouth of horse A is simply formed by carving a channel with the ⅛in, 3mm No.10. Then slightly round over the edges of the mouth. First define the open mouth of horse B with the ⅛in, 3mm No.10 down to a depth of about ¹⁄₁₆in, 2mm.

The wood in the centre can be removed with a hacksaw blade, which has been narrowed by grinding. Then cut out a small V between each tooth with a craft knife.

The mane – It is usual for a horse's mane to fall mainly on one side of the neck and this is how it should be depicted for absolute realism. If you decide to carve the mane in this manner, you should depict the large prominent muscle that follows the graceful curve of the neck on the bare side, which is concealed by mane on the carving illustrated. My preference is for lots of beautiful flowing hair, so I have allowed myself a bit of artistic license here.

Clean up the surface of the neck with a scraper and then mark on the main hanks of hair as shown in the drawing. Note one of the main hanks of horse B's hair flows over the right front leg of horse A, and horse B has a small tendril of hair flowing across the cheek.

Deeply define the edges of each main hank of hair with a ⅜in, 10mm No.10 and then draw on each of them two or three diagonal lines which flow smoothly from one side of each hank to the other. Define these but not quite so deeply with a ¼in, 6mm No.9.

Then make a series of small random cuts with ¹⁄₁₆in, 2mm No.10, carefully following the natural flow of the hair on all the bare surfaces. The tail

....
Details of the muscles, and pronounced, flaring nostrils

can be carved in the same way, except the gouge cuts should be much longer.

THE MUSCLES

Draw on all the muscles as shown in the drawing and define them quite deeply with a ¼in, 6mm No.9, removing the waste wood surrounding them with a ¼in, 6mm No.3 so the muscles stand proud. They can then be contoured smoothly into the surrounding legs with a small scraper.

Small scrapers are not commercially available as far as I know, but they can be made up easily by hacksawing a tapering strip from a cabinet scraper approximately ⅜in, 10mm at one end and about ¼in, 6mm at the other. The ends are then filed or ground round. They can then be sharpened in the conventional way, although with a little more difficulty.

THE BASE

The lower edge of the hooves cannot be rounded properly and finished off until the top surface of the base has been levelled, so this is a good time to complete the base.

Finished rear view of horse A. I cut small hollows at the back of the hooves.

There are many ways of carving the base. For example, as an alternative to the one illustrated, you could make one irregularly shaped with rocks protruding from it and perhaps some vegetation carved across the top surface.

To carve the illustrated base, you should now level the top surface by making a series of smooth, shallow slicing cuts across with a very sharp ⅜in, 10mm No.6, all following in the same direction. These gouge marks can then be left in the finished work to provide a contrast between the polished sides and the subject.

The cove which is formed around the top edge was cut in with a router but if you do not have one, you could cut in with a ¼in, 6mm No.9 The slight irregularities which are inevitably left can be smoothed out either with a rat tail file or a piece of sandpaper wrapped round a length of dowel of a suitable diameter.

The base sides are not easy to finish to the high standard required, as the grain runs across them. Make every effort to get them as smooth as possible. The centre of one of the polished sides would be a good place to make your mark.

I cut mine in with the tip of a sharp craft knife. I find the Stanley Slim knife is ideal for this purpose as, unlike most craft knife blades, the Stanley blades are stout enough to take reasonable sideways force without snapping.

With the top surface of the base finished, the hooves can now be rounded and the small hollows at the back of the hooves cut in. Stab down vertically with a ¼in, 6mm No.9 and then remove the chip with a ⅛in, 3mm No.3. I hollowed out the bottom of the visible hooves of horse A like a normal hoof, although I don't think it added to the realism in any way and could well be omitted.

THE FINISHING

Scrape out all the remaining gouge marks except for the top surface of the base and then sand with reducing grades of sandpaper, finishing with about 600 grit wet and dry. The sanding will show up slightly rough areas which you have missed previously, and these can now be sanded.

Do not attempt to sand the manes and tails, but you can clean them up. Hacksaw a ¾in, 20mm long slot in the end of a ¼in, 6mm rod (a 4in, 100mm nail with the head cut off will do) then insert a 3 x ¾in, 75 x 20mm length of 600 grit wet and dry in the slot.

When this is revolved at high speed in an electric drill, it will clean up the manes without rounding over crisply carved edges, if used with restraint.

It is advantageous to fold the wet and dry in half along its length, both to stiffen it and to present two sanding surfaces instead of one. A few short cuts should also be made in each end to provide fingers which will penetrate into the recesses in the manes.

With the sanding complete, rub the carving down vigorously with a lint-free cloth. This will not only remove the dust but also burnish the wood in preparation for the sealer.

Coat the whole carving, including, the bottom of the base, with sanding sealer, or with Melamine finish which will serve the same purpose but is also impervious to accidental water staining. When thoroughly dry, sand down the easy to sand areas with the well worn wet and dry, using the drill to denib the manes and tails.

Some areas are impossible to clean up to a high standard, and these should be resealed and left. Finally polish with a good quality wax polish until you have worked up a lovely soft lustre. ●

Reg Parsons' interest in woodcarving stemmed from his father, a talented woodcarver and artist. Reg's work has covered a wide spectrum from pub signs and ships' figureheads to church statuary, but his main interest has always been carving animals. Reg teaches at adult education classes in Cornwall and hopes to encourage others to take up the craft which has given him so much pleasure.

HEAD ABOVE THE REST

JOHN HOYLE DISCUSSES HIS CARVING OF AN UNUSUAL GREEN MAN

Not another green man! You may think we have enough of that fraternity around already. And, yes, the woodcarving world is certainly not short of pre-Christian sylvan deities, or foliate men as they are sometimes called.

The only good reason for carving another, in the face of so many, is the design. It is a brilliant design, and I can say so because although I carved his head, I did not design it. I wish I had. The unknown man responsible has been dead for around 700 years.

Although he is long gone, his green man lives on, wary, opportunist, knowing and lecherous, as a sculpted corbel supporting a wall-mounted statue in Bamburg cathedral, Bavaria. The statue, called the *Bamburg Rider*, has been there since 1259, so I expect the design is no longer subject to copyright.

I recommend this design because I think it retains enough of the wild, secretive sensuality that a pre-Christian deity should have, without becoming the fearful mass of burgeoning and decay which makes some medieval foliate men so powerfully repulsive.

The development of the Bamburg man, from face to foliage, is delicately done and leads the observer from eyelid to leaf or from beard to branch without shock, while leaving the impression of bone and sinew beneath.

Many of the Bamburg man's foliate fellows, decorating corbels and bosses all over Europe, are more rampantly verdant with leaves and branches exploding

Above **Drawing of the Bamburg green man corbel**
Below **Close-up of the finished green man showing the cavities**
Below right **The finished green man**

from ears, nostrils and mouth, and even from blind eye sockets. At the other extreme, there are many modern green men carved in shallow relief, very flat and bland, resembling a sunburst with a face in it, and with as much secretive sensuality as a pot duck.

The Bamburg green man was a stone corbel and I have transformed him into a boss, because I wanted to hang him on my wall. Although the boss form allowed most of the carving to be done flat on the bench, I needed to have it in a vertical hold to finish the crown and chin.

I carved him from a block of limewood (*Tilia vulgaris*) measuring 14 x 13 x 5in, 355 x 330 x 125mm. The use of wood allowed me to add detail to the original flattened acanthus leaf form, and surely no material could have been more suitable for a sylvan deity!

Although the carving was uneventful, I found the large burrs, used for creating the 36 undercut cavities, a bit hair-raising. After sanding from 80 to 360 grit I sealed the carving with two coats of sanding sealer. I rubbed it down with 1, 000 wire wool and then finished with wax. He now hangs on my wall, illuminated by a single spotlight. ●

SITTING PRETTY

PETER TREE EXPLAINS HOW TO CARVE CLASSIC BACK SPLAT CHAIRS

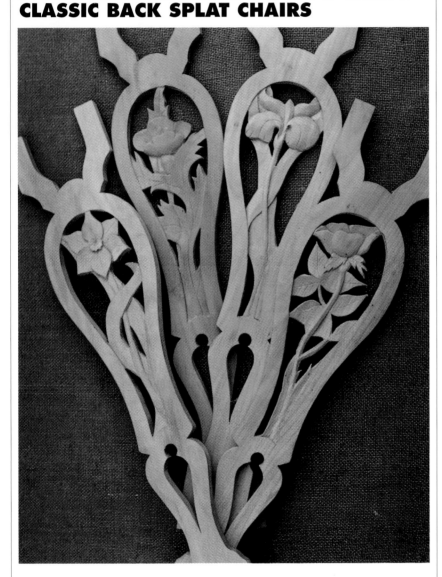

Set of flowers, daffodil, poppy, iris, dog rose

Variations of almost all popular patterns of Windsor chair incorporate a black splat or baluster in their design. Chairs with back splats aren't significantly stronger than their all-spindle relatives, so the function must be decorative. Perhaps it allows the chairmaker to create a pleasing focal point for his work.

Back splats appear in many shapes and sizes, often being known by specific names such as Fiddle, Bulls Eye, Christmas Tree and Wheelback. Others are interpretations of designs commonly associated with a particular period. Some are fretted out and carved as commemorative devices. The back splats I carve and build into chairs are, I feel, my contribution to this long tradition of diversity.

I design the carvings usually in sets of six which have a common theme, such as fruits and leaves of trees, British flora. My favourite set is based on aspects of conservation, and has a frog featured in one panel which is always fun to carve, and for some reason often ends up with a hint of a grin.

Choosing a subject suitable for a panel design needs care. It should have a definite recognisable form which won't be upset by the confines of the panel shape, or be lost after some stylisation. Ideally the set should also be made up of images that have a similar scale in real life, as disproportion in a set can look clumsy.

I transfer each design onto stiff card and cut it out to make a working template, which is used in conjunction with a master template for the whole splat. Sometimes I brush the cards with a coat of varnish which helps to extend their working life.

WOOD CHOICE

Fine-grained woods are usually stronger in small section than some more open-grained woods used in chair construction. Bold grain could interrupt the appearance of a finished carving and actually reduce the visual impact.

For these reasons I carve the back splats (unless working to a special request) in what are loosely termed fruitwoods. I like using apple (*Malus sylvestris*), cherry (*Prunus spp.*), holly (*Ilex spp.*) and pear (*Pyrus communis*), but my personal favourite is hawthorn (*Crataegus spp.*)

It has a wonderful, fine grain, smooth texture and often displays quite subtle colouring. Hawthorn carves like a dream, which more than compensates for the problem of availability. So far though, I've always been lucky enough to maintain a reasonable stock level.

I've found my customers have a genuine interest in the woods I use to build a chair, and are delighted to own furniture containing rarely seen timbers.

FALLEN FOREST

Over the last couple of years I have also been carving some bog yew (*Taxus baccata*). I collect this from a site which must have been an impressive forest roughly around the time of our Bronze Age, some 3,500 years ago.

The location in the Fens is now arable farmland. It is a serious problem for the local farmers, as some of the trunks can weigh up to a couple of tons, and lie buried just beneath the surface. I've seen a ploughing tractor stopped dead in its tracks on hitting one, luckily not breaking any equipment on that occasion.

Interestingly, nearly all of the yews, and a few oaks as well, lie in the same direction, perhaps indicating they were uprooted together during a storm or flood. The wood from these ancient yews is often quite sound, but suffers badly from checking and splitting as it dries. It's heavier and a lot tougher than ordinary yew, with a darker appearance, and gives off a strange fusty odour when sawn or sanded.

Because of its liability to crack, only relatively small pieces are eventually usable, seldom enough for a whole backsplat. So I make up composites, using maybe cherry for the surround and bog yew inserted for the panel area.

Bog yew aside, local home-grown timber yards are the best source of wood for back splat material. When they are available I have a green log of suitable timber slash-sawn to $\frac{5}{8}$in, 15mm thick. This allows enough leeway for me to plane both sides and thickness to the finished size of $\frac{7}{16}$in, 11mm. The boards are carefully seasoned using thin, closely-spaced stickers, covered and weighted down.

PROFILE CUTS

I begin the carved back splats with the seasoned, thickenessed material, using the templates to mark out their whole shapes and the areas to be carved. I drill the waste portions to allow a fretsaw blade to be threaded through.

My fretsaw machine, an Oliver, is quite old, having a flatbelt drive with a clutch mechanism which makes stopping and starting during blade changing an easy operation. Originally it had a crossbow arrangement made from a lath of ash (*Fraxinus spp*) as a return spring, which I've now replaced with something similar to catapult elastic.

The blades I use are snapped off lengths of fine-tooth $\frac{1}{8}$in, 3mm bandsaw blade. These are just small enough for the job, they cut freely and leave a fairly smooth edge. It's worth spending a little extra time at the fret saw to ensure the profile is cut as accurately and cleanly as possible before the carving starts.

....

Left **Drilling a backsplat to allow a fret saw blade to be threaded through**
Top right **Fretsaw with cardboard templates of the carvings**
Right **A splat bolted on to the carving stand**

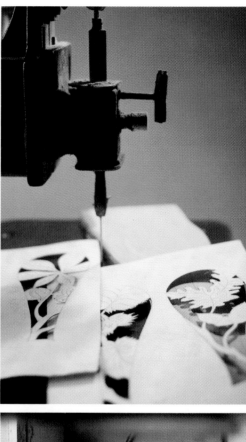

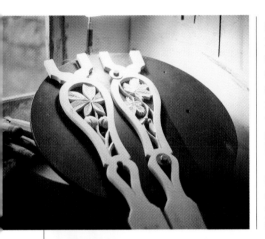

SPECIAL STAND

My carving stand is purpose-built to enable easy access from all sides of the carved piece. Basically it is a turntable, set at an angle of about 30°. The table is an old, heavy lathe face-plate, 18in, 460mm in diameter with a base which sits snugly into an inclined wooden block and is free to rotate.

Because of the face-plate's mass, movement is not a problem while carving even when using a mallet, and yet it can be relatively easily rotated to negotiate cuts from any direction.

The pre-fretted back splats are gripped to the table with a couple of bolts and large washers. I place a ⅛in, 3mm pad of hard rubber between the wood and hard metal to stop any possibility of a carving tool's edge hitting the steel. Just the thought is enough to make any carver shudder.

The upper working end of the stand is set firmly into a heavy base making an overall height of around 40in, 1015mm. This is comfortable to work at standing or sitting on a high stool. I've fixed an adjustable lamp behind the stand, which is angled to cast a glancing ray of light that picks out carved detail as the work progresses.

First cuts are made to the carved panel by vertically setting in the perimeter lines with shallow sweep gouges, relieving the cut at its inside edge. Then quite rapidly I remove the larger areas of waste with gouges and mallet, often alternating with a V tool to outline major detail. Where possible I try to complete the surface relief of simpler features of leaves and stems.

Even though the work is taking shape fairly quickly, careful cuts are essential, the work-piece is fragile and could be split easily by too heavy a blow or by a chopping cut along the grain. Damage is almost impossible to repair and would waste not only the wood but also time and effort invested to reach this stage.

DETAIL

When the roughing out is complete, I put the mallet aside, unless the particular pattern being carved features a cluster of berries. These are a real pleasure to carve with the correct technique.

I use a deep-throated gouge with an internal width which matches the diameter of the berry. I start the cut almost horizontally, half way across the

Top left **The carving turntable**
Left **Cleaning up the carving with a long pointed skew**

fruit, and then gradually raise it with light taps from the mallet until it reaches an upright position.

After repeating the action from the opposite direction, a clean-cut half sphere should be the result. I carve more berries as necessary, maybe leaving fragments of debris between them until later.

TRUSTY TOOLS

Carving detail takes different amounts of time to complete, depending upon the complexity of the design, but usually between 20 and 30 minutes.

The tools I use are a standard set, with a few exceptions. Having turned wood for many years with High Speed Steel tools, and noted their advantages, I've now made several carving tools from the same material.

Some use readily available HSS turning tool blades which are re-ground to an edge suitable for carvings, but others, like a skew, a shallow fish-tailed gouge, and a particularly useful whittling-type knife, I fashioned from disused planer blades.

I am the first to admit HSS is not the easiest stuff to grind into any shape, but with care and a lot of patience a super tool is the reward, able to take a razor-sharp edge that will outlast many times a more conventional carbon-steel tool.

To maintain a cutting edge on carving tools, and incidentally on all of my turning tools, I use what can only be described as a rotary strop, a 6in, 150mm diameter disc of hard leather mounted onto the arbour of a fractional horsepower motor running at 1450rpm, dressed with fine valve grinding paste. Tools are drawn across the running surface, easily removing grinding burrs, and leaving a sharp polished edge.

As the carving is nearing completion I use a tiny V tool to add the leaf veins. Some patterns may need a little work with shaped punches to define detail. Horse-chestnuts for

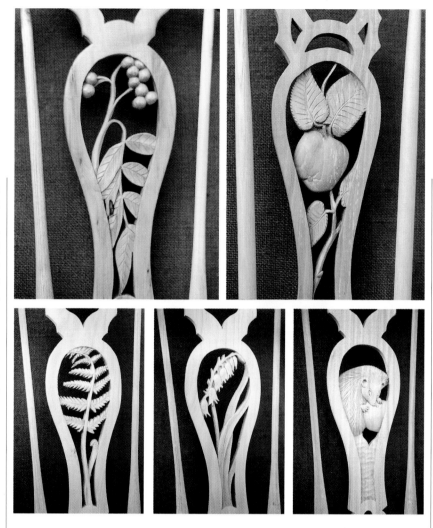

Clockwise from top left
Rowan, Apple, Hedgehog, Bluebell, Fern

....

instance, have the suggestion of spines impressed into the surface.

FINISHING

Cleaning up the carvings can be done with a long pointed skew, but I especially like to use a scalpel. The blade's slight flexibility helps get into tight corners, and can be made to flow around either internal or external contours while taking off a very fine slice. Straight edge blades seem to work best.

Finally, I lightly sand the carvings with a shop-made abrasive mop held in a pillar drill. The mop is made from torn ribbons of 320 grit cloth, about 4in, 100m long x ½in, 12mm wide, and hole punched in the middle.

About 30 are threaded randomly onto an arbour and trapped with a nut and washers. The sanding is a compromise, it does slightly round off crisp detail, but at an acceptable level. I have to ensure there are no sharp edges which might snag a sitter's clothing.

The first chairs I made with carved splats were commissioned for an exhibition about ten years ago, and promptly sold on the opening day. They were the realisation of a flight of fancy, which over the years has developed into the mainstay of a distinctive range of avidly collected classic chairs. ●

Peter Tree has been carving for pleasure since childhood, encouraged by a small carving set he was given for Christmas. He still has those treasured tools and uses them often. They have taken him through whittling firewood as a boy to the delicate images he now carves on the chairs he makes for a living.

⬤ SUPERBOWL

TECHNIQUE

CHARLES MILLER TELLS HOW HE MADE A BALL AND SOCKET WORKHOLDER USING A BOWLING BALL

When looking for a suitable carving holding device, I was amazed at the prices charged for good quality machines. So I tried a less expensive approach and made my own versatile workholder. It holds a carving firmly and allows rotation of 360° on two axes, standing immobile against the hardest of mallet blows.

In the USA we have a bowling game called duck pins. I'm sure there is a British equivalent (perhaps skittles). The ball used is approximately 5in, 125mm in diameter and does not have thumb or finger holes. I scrounged a damaged ball from a bowling alley.

The component parts of the workholder.

My first step was to drill a 2½in, 63mm diameter countersink hole in the ball to a depth of about ¾in, 20mm. I drilled a second hole the same diameter and depth at the antipodes of the first.

Centred on the countersink, I then drilled a 1¼in, 32mm hole all the way through the ball. I now had a hole completely drilled through with countersink spaces at each end.

I chose to drill a hole 1¼in, 32mm across because I had a 13in, 330mm piece of 1¼in, 32mm all-thread rod (studding) which needed a good home. I inserted the rod in the drilled hole and fixed it in place with epoxy paste.

I positioned the rod with one end flush with the ball's surface, the other extending about 8in, 200mm on the other side. I then tightened 1¼in, 32mm nuts on each side, one side flush with the ball's surface. The countersink voids were then filled and smoothed with epoxy paste.

Next I sawed and ground a 5in, 125mm tapering section from the end of the rod. To this I affixed a 6 x 2½ x ¾in, 150 x 63 x 20mm wooden platform. This meant I had to drill two holes in the rod to receive wood screws. The screws plus a bed of epoxy held the wooden platform in place quite firmly.

It would have been just as easy to leave the rod whole, without a taper, and affix a platform at the end. However, I had this very sturdy and expensive Stubai carver's screw which I could not have used without a tapered section.

I drilled three holes of different sizes through the platform to allow me to use three different sizes of carver's screws.

I intended to grip the ball in the jaws of a vice. To do this I needed two pieces of 9 x 5½ x 1½in, 230 x 140 x 38mm wood. I had some ordinary soft pine (*Pinus*) and cut a 4½ x 1¼in, 115 x 32mm notch in each piece, allowing them to drop into place and remain in place between the vice jaws.

Then came the hard part. A concavity was needed in each auxiliary vice jaw to match the convex surface of the ball. This could have been prepared easily with machines I do not possess. A Delta radial arm drill would have been a simple approach.

To do the job with hand tools I first wasted away a large bit of wood from the two blocks by drilling. Then I began with gouges. After approximating the depth, I sandwiched the ball and the two wood pieces in the vice and

The workholder in use. It can be swivelled to any angle.

placed some carbon paper between the ball and wood with the carbon faced toward the wood.

Tightening the vice gently, I rotated the ball. This made black marks on the proud spots which needed more trimming. Then I carved off the blackened spots and repeated the process until I had wooden surfaces which matched the ball.

The height of my workholder is 45in, 1145mm from the floor to the tip of the rod (my bench height is 35in, 890mm). As I remain seated for most of my whittling the height of the workholder is just right.

The ball and socket held in a vice is also explained in Reg Parsons' book *Woodcarving – A Manual of Techniques*. ●

Stubai tools are available from The Working Tree, Milland, Nr Liphook, Hants GU30 7JS.
Tel: 01428 741 672

For details of UK stockists of Delta tools write to:
Westwings House, Station Road, Guiseley, West Yorkshire LS20 8BX
Tel: 01943 873 535

TIDY TOOLS

PETER JARVIS TELLS HOW HE MADE A SPACE-SAVING AND CONVENIENT TOOL RACK

I have enjoyed many holidays in the Ziller valley in the Austrian Tyrol. It was always a pleasure to visit the local shops, existing only to produce and sell woodcarvings, and to talk to the carvers working in public view at their benches.

While looking round these shops, I noticed a tiered tool rack next to each work station, stoutly made out of heavy timbers. Each tool was readily to hand in its own slot, separated from its neighbour.

When setting up my own workshop there was much less room to play with, as it was only a garden shed measuring 8 x 6ft, 2.4 x 1.8m. It also had to house all my gardening tools and equipment, a Kity 613 bandsaw, grinding wheel, Koch carvers clamp on

its own bench and other tools which I had accumulated over a lifetime.

I had a number of Terry spring clips and two magnetic tool holders, as well as dresser hooks, screws and nails which were used to hold as many articles as possible making them quickly available.

That was not enough, as I also needed room to put all my carving gouges neatly in one place, so I fixed up a shelf with three rows of holes over the main workbench.

When the carving clamp was installed on the other side of the shed, it became a chore to have to turn round to use or replace each tool, so I needed to make something more appropriate.

I had a number of 4ft, 1.2m lengths

of ½ x ³⁄₁₆in, 13 x 5mm mild steel strips, so these came in useful for my tool rack.

ACHIEVING ARTICULATION

The original design was for a single swinging arm fastened to the main shed frame, bearing a tray which would hold two dozen or so gouges. But the installation went less than half way to resolving the problems, and several modifications were needed.

First, I needed to make the second arm which had to be articulated. That meant the end of the first arm had to be modified with a curved bracket to hold the swivel pin.

Bending the ends of the bracket to one side had the advantage of enabling the arms to be folded on to one another without interfering with each other at the hinge point.

The double arm and rack of tools

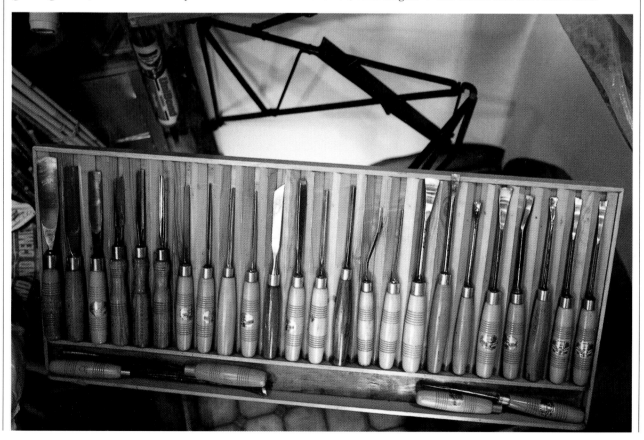

For maximum flexibility I mounted the tray on to the arm using a steel pin inserted into a brass insert in a wooden block. This was attached by a hinge to the centre of the underside of the tray. The whole rack was controllable to any angle through about 90° by means of a friction stay.

The tray was a board, edged and divided by triangular fillets to separate the 24 gouges. My tray was made from an offcut of parana pine (*Pinus spp.*), but you can make your tray from whatever suitable wood you have around. I mention it because when I filled it with tools, and extended it with the two parts of the support arms at right angles, the weight caused the failure of the bolt at the 'X' point of the first arm.

This slight mishap accounts for the appearance of the heavier strut, which was inserted simply enough, being only a piece of 1in, 25mm angle iron retained by one small bolt mounted through the cross over point to absorb the side thrusts. I had to make a slight change to the layout of the basic arm to prevent the weakness caused by the two stage development.

The adaptability of the design meant the tray could be instantly lifted

off its mounting pin, and since the arms were mounted similarly on home-made lift off pin hinges, the whole rack could be dismantled whenever necessary.

OTHER MODIFICATIONS

You will notice from the picture, that I used a second friction stay and this was yet another modification which might, or might not be necessary with a different installation.

However, because of where the structure was fixed, the stay was needed to stop the prime arm from moving to the right under the weight of the tools. By the same token, a restraint might be necessary at the central swivel point, and could be done by tightening a nut on the swivel pin itself, or perhaps by inserting a suitable rubber washer. ●

Above left **Detail of the central swivel joint**
Above **The final mounting point for the tool rack**
Left **The hinged block and stay**

When Peter Jarvis retired from business in 1984 his wife gave him a set of six small gouges, which eventually developed into a comprehensive collection. He is largely self-taught, and now aged 77 he carves as often as possible, producing wildlife and abstract sculptures for sale and for commissions.

MODEL DAUGHTERS

GARRY ARTHUR DESCRIBES HOW PAUL DEANS CARVED PORTRAIT BUSTS OF TWO SISTERS FOR THEIR FATHER

Craftspeople are notoriously hard-up. The enjoyment they get from their craft is not often matched by the monetary rewards, so their spending power is not great. Sometimes the solution is found in the age-old process of barter, and that is what sculptor Paul Deans from Christchurch, New Zealand, proposed when faced with a bill for some expensive orthodontic work on his daughters.

A versatile artist, Paul is in demand as a portrait painter and sketcher as well as for his work as a wood sculptor. The orthodontist talked to Paul about having paintings or drawings made of his two daughters Anna and Elizabeth Glass, aged 17 and 14 respectively.

But when he saw pictures of heads Paul had carved in wood, he asked him to carve their portraits instead. The result is two charming portrait busts in lime (*tilia spp.*) that capture perfectly the girls' serene facial expressions.

....

Carvings of Elizabeth (left) and Anna.

PORTRAIT PREPARATION

An accurate likeness was needed, and Paul began by taking photographs of the girls from all angles. Then he did some detailed drawings, front views, profiles, three-quarters views, and views from above, looking down on their faces.

"I should have taken photos from the back for the hair, and from below the chin too," he says. "That's what I would do if I was doing it again."

When he visited the girls, he took a large pair of callipers and they let him take detailed measurements of their heads and facial details. Each one was noted on a chart which he found in a book, *Modelling a Likeness in Clay*. It has 20 different outline views of the

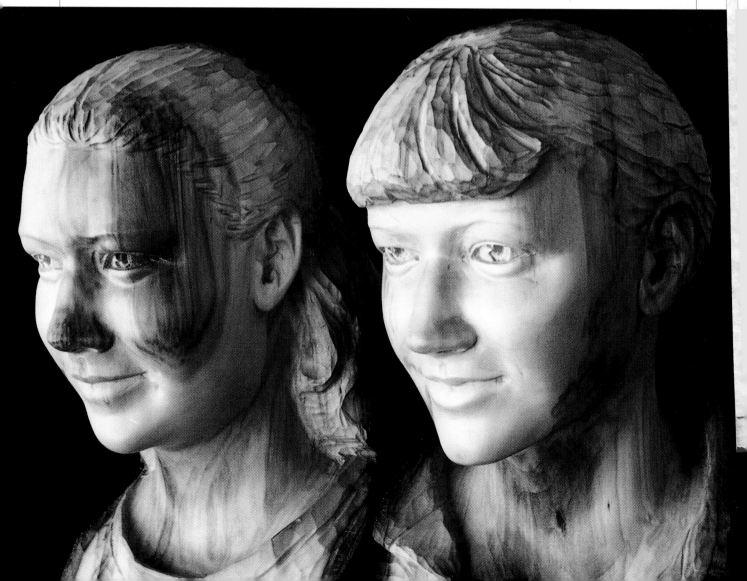

Above **Three-quarters profile of Elizabeth.**
Above right, **Three-quarters profile of Anna.**

Below **Paul shapes the mouth on the carving of Elizabeth.**

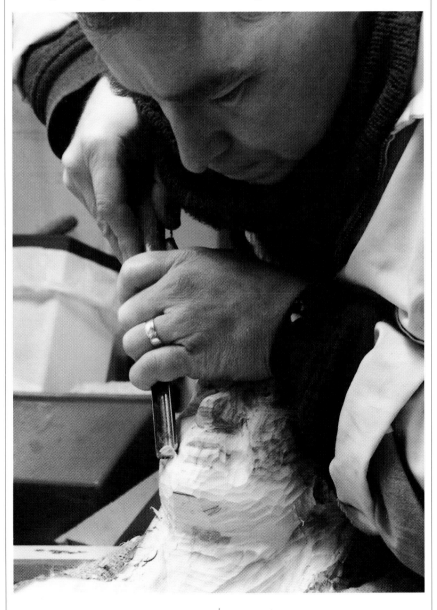

have in a room," he says. "It looks larger than life. It's quite strange." 80% of life-size was his original intention, but he found the lime log was not quite big enough. As it was, at 75%, he just managed to fit the ears in.

He had the log for two years before carving. It proved to have brown colour in it, contrasting with the typical cream, but he decided this was not bad enough to cause a problem. His client liked the idea of leaving the bark near the base of each sculpture.

Next, Paul drew each head to scale using the measurements he had taken. The son of a professional painter, he has done a lot of portrait sketching himself as a way of earning a living. He studied industrial design at Wellington Polytechnic, and found life drawing the highlight of the week.

He is convinced an ability to draw is a great asset when carving portraits. "I study faces," he says. "When you become aware of the problem areas you are working on, you look at people's faces and observe how they work."

All that groundwork, the photographs, the measurements, the scale drawings, eventually gave Paul all the information he needed. "You can do all the preparation," he says, "but there comes a time when you've got to take a deep breath and make a start."

ROUGHING OUT

Ready at last to take tools to the wood, he cleaned off a flat front of the first log, marked the positions of the chin and the nose, and began to work back from there. Using the chainsaw (which he found pretty scary) he cut back to the hairline, then he cut to the correct depth under the nose and under the chin.

To ensure consistent results, he took each sculpture to a certain stage, then stopped and did the same to the other one. Rough shaping of the main proportions of the entire head came next, using a large No 7 gouge and a deep No 10.

head on which to mark measurements, most of them using the little round lump at the front of the ear as a reference point.

Paul found his sitters remarkably co-operative. "I probably found the procedure more embarrassing than they did," he recalls. "It's a very intimate thing to do to anyone's face."

He scaled all the measurements down to three-quarters life-size. "A full-scale head is quite dominating to

Paul generously shared his knowledge with a group of woodcarvers from the Canterbury Guild of Woodworkers. He had a rapt audience as he demonstrated, on a head he had roughed out from another chunk of lime, just how he carved the eyes, nose, mouth and ears of the Glass girls. This was his advice:

THE EYES

Having left the bulge where the eye fits in, mark out the opening and cut in along the line with a small, shallow gouge. Then cut back to the eyeball shape, remembering the eyeball is a sphere. Between the eyebrow and the eyelid there is usually a bulge or fold that should be allowed for.

Define the actual form of the eyelid, with the bottom lid slightly tucked under at the ends. The iris can be carved as a raised disc on the eyeball, or as a round depression. Paul carved the little depression for the pupil quite deeply.

Avoid a staring effect by not showing the whole circle of the iris. Leave the top of it under the eyelid.

Leave a small round or V-shape in the iris for the little point of light, the highlight, which you see in people's eyes.

THE NOSE

The wings of the nose must be carved back from where the nose meets the lip. The outer edges of the wings of the nose are in line with the inside corners of the eyes.

THE MOUTH

Carve the overall shape over the mouth and lips together, remembering the mouth is not straight across, but curves around the teeth. The same applies to the whole face, which is not flat, but curves right back to the ears.

Cut straight into the line where the lips join, then carve the shape of the lips. There is no definite edge to the lips with most people. It's the colour change that we see, not a physical change.

THE EARS

Leave a block for the ears. The main thing to remember is the ear is not quite upright, it leans back. And the back of the ear is further out from the head.

There are some almost universal proportions which are helpful in blocking out the face. For example:

● The eyes are positioned halfway between the crown of the head and the chin.
● The distance between the pupils of the eyes is generally the same as the distance from the chin to the bottom of the nose, the bottom of the nose to the eyebrows, and the eyebrows to the hairline.
● The tops and bottoms of the ears line up with the eyebrows and the bottom of the nose.
● Lines joining the pupils and the bottom of the nose form an equilateral triangle.
● Lines joining the back of the ear, the outside tip of the eye, and the bottom of the chin form an equal-sided right-angle triangle.
● The neck, seen from the side, does not come straight up, but comes forward on an angle.

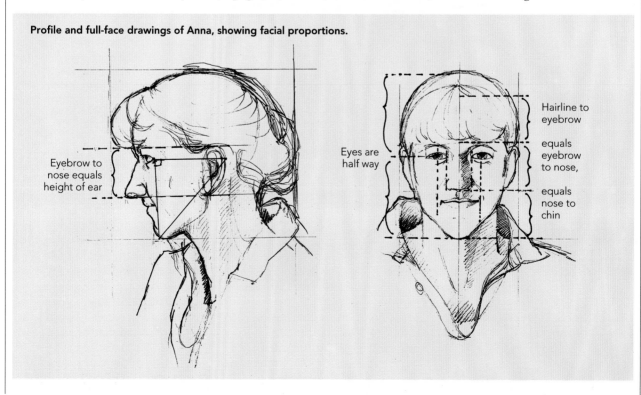

Profile and full-face drawings of Anna, showing facial proportions.

Eyebrow to nose equals height of ear

Eyes are half way

Hairline to eyebrow

equals eyebrow to nose,

equals nose to chin

Paul describes the next step as "sorting out". This involved taking the face back so the nose was left prominent, making allowances for the eyes and the mouth, and carving the general shape of the face right back to the ears. Not to the exact final measurements, but "leaving a bit of meat."

SECOND SITTING

This produced the basic facial framework to be refined down to the measured shapes and sizes. When Paul had the eyes, mouth and other facial features roughed out, he asked the two girls back to re-measure their faces.

"There were some bits I'd missed out on the charts," he says. "It was good to have the girls there at that stage because I could see so much more than I could pick up from the photographs.

"They were tickled pink at seeing recognisable likenesses of themselves, but they were self-conscious about such things as the size of their noses. I had to reassure them it was just because we never see our own noses in profile, and they always look wrong to us."

Bust of Elizabeth with drawings, photographs and measurement chart.

From that point, it was a matter of refining the carved features and getting the hair to look right. Paul left a tooled finish on the hair and the clothing, but went on to wet-sand the skin surfaces down to 400 grit wet-and-dry emery paper.

"With lime you can do the final finish with wet sanding, and it won't fuzz, unlike some other woods," Paul says. Then he oiled the sculptures with Penetrol before a final waxing with Liberon, and buffing to a satisfactory glow.

DEFINING CHARACTER

To reproduce the girls' distinctive expressions, Paul made an intense study of the photographs. "Anna is much leaner in the face and has a more clearly defined jawline," he says, "but in the measure-

Finished carvings of Elizabeth (left) and Anna. Photos by Paul Deanes.

ments they were very, very similar.

"Defining the character becomes a very subtle thing, but as I worked to the measurements I'd taken, I just found them I suppose. Their mouths are quite similar, but Elizabeth is more round in the cheeks. It is in the profiles that the two are most different, especially the noses."

A realistic portrait head is not like an impressionistic or interpretative portrait. It must be a recognisably true likeness of the subject. Paul Deans achieved this to everyone's satisfaction, not only through his undoubted skill as a wood sculptor but also through his painstaking attention to measurements and proportions. ●

New Zealand journalist Garry Arthur has a special interest in writing about arts and crafts. He is also a woodcarver, and has become known for his sculpted furniture using giant carved human hands as holding devices, in seats, tables, lamps and other pieces. Now he's moving on to other body parts!

SLICE OF HISTORY

PHIL TOWNSEND DESCRIBES HOW HE CARVED A HIGH RELIEF MEMORIAL OF A LOCAL HISTORICAL FIGURE

I was commissioned to design and create a memorial, a few years ago, of a local poet who had died a century before. It filled a large, bow-topped window in a public building, and centred on a life-sized portrait carved in high relief. Surrounding it were five pyrography panels which provided a mixture of relevant illustration and text about the poet's life and work.

Close-up of the completed carving

A week or so after the unveiling, an elderly lady called to me from her doorstep to congratulate me on the memorial window, but more importantly to tell me I'd done the wrong man. For an awful moment I wondered if the photo I'd used for the portrait could have been of someone else, but then she asked if I had heard of Jacob Readshaw.

From my confused expression she must have realised I had not. She produced a couple of yellowed newspaper cuttings and spread them on the table. "That's him," she said, "The Genius of Teesdale."

This was my introduction to an almost forgotten Victorian figure, who had been known, the newspaper said, by this rather grandiose title. Elsewhere he was colourfully described as "the bearded, frock-coated wizard".

Though hardly a genius in the contemporary sense, this accolade was understandable in the context of the time and place in which he lived. For Jacob Readshaw combined unusually wide-ranging interests with remarkable talent and a pioneering spirit, a rare mix given the time in which he lived.

A carpenter and joiner by trade, Readshaw was also a cabinet maker, a musician and maker of violins, an oil painter, a Methodist preacher, a professional photographer and a keen amateur astronomer who ground his own lenses and built his own observatory. Furthermore, the lady informed me, he also carved wood, and I went down to the local church to see some of his work.

What I saw there got me interested in researching the life and times of Jacob Readshaw, and eventually resulted in a second commemorative display. The method I used for carving it is explained in this article.

DESIGN

I used the photograph from the newspaper cutting as a basis for the carving. Dressed in his frock coat, with a high starched collar under a moustache-less beard, his hairline was receding but had a wild, windblown appearance around the sides. The mouth was gentle and the eyes had a faraway look.

Having biscuit-jointed three lime (*Tilia vulgaris*) boards to make up the 27in, 685mm width, I sketched a drawing, based on the photograph, on

Above **The design sketched and bandsawed on the block**
Below **I used a router to isolate the left hand and under the beard**

Left **It became apparent there was not enough depth to do the torso justice**
Below **I added a ¾in, 20mm piece to the back of the head to give extra depth**

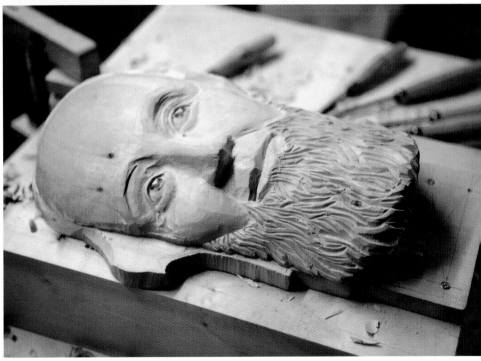

to the surface. To create interest in the pose, I drew him holding a large lens in his left hand while his right hand grasped the edge of his coat (a stance often associated with Victorian gentry), a rolled up chart was held in the angle of his right arm.

The centre board was a little thicker than the other ones, as this was the area in which the greatest depth of carving would lie. I used a bandsaw to cut out the outline of the sketch.

DEEP CUTS

Next, I plunged in with a router to isolate the left arm, hand and the lens, and to cut around the underside of the beard. Using a 1½in, 38mm alongee gouge with a shallow bend, I removed the bulk of the waste, tapering from the right to the left side (which was further from the viewpoint) and chopping up

to the router cut so the wood was cleanly removed.

I also used the router to outline the nose and leading eyebrow. I chopped the face back roughly, leaving the nose tip, left cheekbone and edge of the beard uncut. These were the areas nearest the viewpoint.

At this roughing out stage I could see I had probably overdone the depth of router cut around the hand. It left

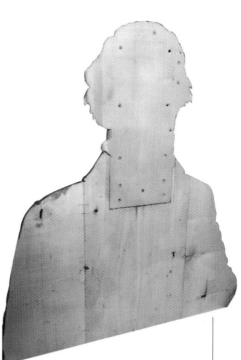

Above **Making a glove fit for the new torso proved slow work. The ¾in, 20mm addition to the head was rough-carved to blend in**
Above right **The ¾in board was glued and screwed to the rear of the head and five lower screws fixed it to the new torso**

too little depth at the central chest area, from which all the rest of the upper torso receded. I decided to concentrate on the head in the hope I would see a way of resolving the problem with the chest, as the carving progressed.

While carving the head I encountered problems again caused by incautious use of the router, this time under Readshaw's left eyebrow. I had gone so deep the other eye had to be cut right back to the limit to leave the left one looking the closer of the two, and even then the sense of depth was less than convincing.

Another problem was the unruly lock of hair on Readshaw's right which I wanted to retain, as it added extra life to the portrait. The point at which this hair actually joined the head was out of view, behind the far side of the head. This had been carved back to what was almost a feather edge, leaving the wood fragile where the lock of hair joined it.

In other respects the head wasn't too bad, but I kicked myself for not starting with deeper timber, which would have allowed easier resolution of these problems. When I re-appraised the rather concave looking chest area I considered scrapping the whole thing and starting again.

In the end I compromised and decided to retain the head, on which I had spent the most time, and replant it on to a new, deeper torso. I knew it was going to be tricky to do without a joint line being evident, but reasoned if I cut round the underside of the beard at an angle with a coping saw, then the majority of the joint might be hidden by the beard's edge.

NEW TORSO

Jacob Readshaw was tried, found guilty and beheaded. I then beefed up the salvaged part with a ¾in, 20mm board, glued and screwed to the rear. The board extended several inches below the head to provide a means of fixing it to the new body. The original lock of hair was removed and I made allowance for it in the added board.

While the head was fixed down to the bench by screws through the square extension, I progressed with the left hand side, which I cut back again to give an increased sense of depth. I cut back the beard under the far cheekbone and the right ear was pushed further away to increase the modelling on that side.

The new torso was an inch thicker and I had to think of a way to get a glove fit between it and the head. This turned out to be a mixture of quick initial removal of stock (cutting out a curve I judged to be near the angle of the underside of the beard) followed by lengthy and tedious paring off and

trying for fit. I coated the underside of the beard in red chalk and wherever that left a red smudge, I thinly removed the surface.

If there are other ways of achieving a glove fit, I hope someone will let me know as I've no wish to repeat the process. It took a full day's work to achieve an acceptable, almost perfect match.

I made a recess for the neck extension and then screwed, rather than glued, the head through the extension into the torso from the rear. This allowed me to remove the head to make carving around and under the beard more accessible.

With this in place, I turned my attention to the new, deeper torso. To reduce the waste removed, I used a piece of lime which was about ¾in, 20mm less in depth for the left hand side, as it was all judged to be receding from view.

PERFECT POSE

Once more I outlined the edge of the leading arm, hand and lens with the router, but this time more judiciously. I altered the object carried under the other arm from a rolled up chart to a book, because a circular object (the lens) was already included in the pose and a rectangular book seemed to give a better balance.

Another cut with the router isolated the lower hand, the position of which was still uncertain, and yet another to ease waste removal between the book and lapels of the jacket. I cut the shoulders right back on their top

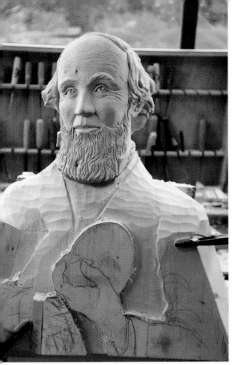  

Above **Carving the neck and shoulder area, with the left hand side chopped right back**
Above centre **The lower hand was cut square and flat to allow lamination of a block to create more depth**
Above right **The completed carving prior to staining**
Right **The joint line between the head and body lies on the upper edge of the bow-tie and under the beard**

edge and removed the waste by working across the grain in a slow curve around the chest, cutting back to a depth of about 1½in at the point where the book meets the armpit.

I sawed the book into shape and drew lines on the top face. First I cut a wedge off so the end face of the book receded from right to left, then the back of the book was tenon-sawn along the far line, followed by chops up to the saw cut with a chisel to clear the angle between the book and the arm. The nearmost face of the book would eventually take the title and I cut it flat and true with a broad paring chisel.

I had trouble envisaging the position of Readshaw's right hand and eventually decided on a pose which required more timber than I had allowed for. Once the throat and lapels had been developed and the book and supporting arm worked out, it was evident I would have to laminate on an extra piece to give adequate depth to the knuckles of the hand.

Hands aren't easy parts of the anatomy to carve. While many people find it difficult to draw a life-like hand, anyone can tell you when a hand looks wrong. This is because it's one of the

most familiar parts of the body.

I wasn't satisfied with the final outcome, the hand gripping the coat would have been less fist-like if I'd left the forefinger slightly extended, but it seemed to pass muster with most viewers.

FINISHING TOUCHES
I sanded the skin of the face and hands to increase the contrast of texture between them and the hair and clothing. The title of the book and pamphlet in the breast pocket were burnt in with a pyrograph.

The unruly hair helped to enliven a rather formal Victorian pose. I liked the odd combination of a man who looked well overdue for a haircut and yet sufficiently concerned about his appearance to train some of what he had over his balding skull. The joint line between the tie and the collar was tight enough to go unremarked but perhaps a little too straight.

The next step was to stain the piece to heighten the contrast and increase the realism. I used a sepia water-based stain throughout, in differing dilutions,

Above **Underside view of the carving showing the decrease in depth from left to right**
Below **The completed carving with lunar landscape**

to give a homogenous, monochrome appearance similar to Victorian photographs. I treated the shirt, lens, pamphlet, book end and cuff with wood bleach to extend the process. I also used bleach on the circular device machined into the MDF backing panel, to suggest the surface of the moon.

I incised Jacob Readshaw's name and dates into a block of mahogany in Victorian script. I then gilded the carved lettering and screwed the block from the rear to the backing panel. With the carving similarly fixed from behind and positioned with the head central to the moon's surface, I gave the whole piece a coat of sanding sealer and two coats of hard wax.

PYROGRAPHY PANELS

With the central carving complete, I began work on the five surrounding panels which had to combine relevant illustration and text describing Readshaw's life and works.

I cut windows into each of the MDF panels. These were rounded over on the front edge and rebated on the back to take the birch ply inserts. I burned in the text and illustrations with the excellent Peter Child pyrography machine. This tool maintains sufficient heat for fairly rapid

continuous writing (when you have a large amount of text it can be tedious to work with a low powered unit) and yet stays cool and comfortable in the hand. Pyrography was particularly well-suited to this project, as the colouring was reminiscent of early sepia photographs.

I decided to give every panel a separate theme, each related to a different interest or talent. As Readshaw's main claim to fame was as an amateur astronomer, I chose this subject for the top centre panel with an illustration based on a photograph taken of Readshaw when he was quite elderly, next to his home-made telescope. The long horizontal illustration below depicts his home and workshops.

The corner panels were awkward shapes to fill, but this was resolved by arranging two separate illustrations in each. The left side dealt with his profession as a photographer, showing an early type of camera and

Left **Using the pyrography machine for illustrations and text**
Above **The memorial in situ**

Readshaw's logo, copied from the back of one of his photographs. The right hand corner showed two examples of the finer side of his woodwork, a display cabinet and violin.

The text on the long side panels was relieved by two illustrations on each. The right hand dealt with his main source of income as a joiner and builder, and his life-long devotion to the Methodist Church.

The left hand side gave a brief life history and related some of Readshaw's artistic activities, oil-paintings and ornamental carving, some of which can still be seen in Teesdale today. ●

Phil Townsend's work in high relief has won awards in the International Woodcarvers Congress two years in a row. He usually works in this medium because he believes it allows for a broader choice of subject matter. The manipulation of a limited depth of wood to give the appearance of full 3D is the technique which most intrigues him. He can be contacted for commissions on 01833 640683

Joe Dampf is one of Canada's finest and best known woodcarvers. His carvings have delighted thousands at woodcarving shows in Canada and the United States. Articles about his work have appeared in many woodcarving and woodworking magazines.

For the past 25 years he has developed his method of sculpturing a full-size finished replica of the desired wood carving in clay, from which he meticulously carves an exact duplicate in wood. His artistic talents in forming the clay are matched by his skill in carving the wood, thus producing magnificent carvings, admired by all.

At international woodcarving competitions in North America his carvings have won eight Best of Show awards, four 2nd Best of Show, and three 3rd Best of Show.

Almost fifteen years ago Joe helped organise the Ontario Wood Carvers Association and was president for two years and a director for seven. He was also a director of the American Wood Carvers Congress for six years, and has been teaching in Ontario, Iowa and Pennsylvania for seven.

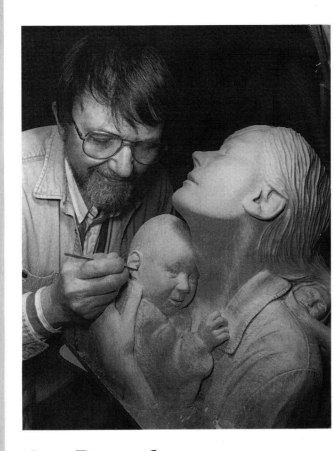

TECHNIQUE

Working Woman
Joe at work on a portrait of his daughter and grandson. He has included two small heads in this piece 'to show the tension to which a woman is subjected when trying to juggle the roles of wife, mother and career person'

Joe Dampf

Modelling in clay before carving in wood is the method favoured by this well-known Canadian carver. Here he describes just what is involved.

Why should I work with clay? Why should I do a piece twice? I win ribbons now for my work! I have my own way of carving, why not just attack the wood and see what develops? Clay is sticky, clammy and messy! I can always use a pattern.

These are some comments and questions that come from my students. Other questions are: **How can I improve my work? I just can't do eyes, or hands and feet. How do I go about making a pattern I can follow?**

For a carver confronted with a large block of wood, doesn't it make sense to do clay studies prior to carving? Composing in clay is better — you can add or subtract, twist and move an arm or leg or head, or relate one figure to another. It is easy to become 3-dimensional in clay. It takes a lot of courage to cut deeply into wood, and this is doubly true if your idea has not been worked out beforehand.

Michelangelo

You are in good company making models. Michelangelo, in his old age, could carve stone directly because he was highly trained in marble pointing from terra cotta models. He always made these models (many full scale) to work from. Pointing off in marble is an ancient measuring technique that employs a sliding needle that measures the depth of the forms. Pointing machines for stone are still sold today in sculpture supply houses.

Some may have reservations about making clay models prior to carving. If you enjoy taking a piece of driftwood or tree branch, and

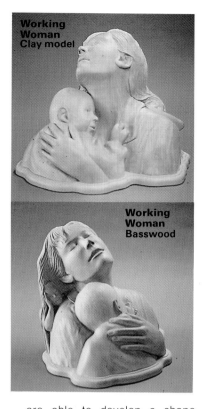

Working Woman Clay model

Working Woman Basswood

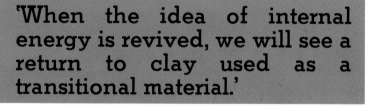

Rocky Mountain High Brasswood. 28" x 36"

It's the Real Thing Mahogany

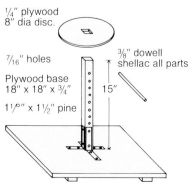

are able to develop a shape inspired by the natural forms suggested, well and good. However 'Truth to materials' is a contemporary notion which has only relative validity and only limited practicality. Abstract art, of course, is the perfect expression of this idea. For all the ideas of organic form and internal space, abstract sculpture is generally concerned with the outward form. The pent-up energy of a Rodin, Michelangelo or the Greeks is a forgotten idea that has been relegated to the past. When and if this idea of internal energy is

My first attempt was to take profile and frontal photos of my son and then enlarge them to lifesize. After glueing these to cardboard and cutting out to the outlines, they were used as templates held against the wood. It wasn't a bad method but it had serious limitations. After a second attempt, I realised I could never achieve the desired results without modelling in clay prior to carving. Now all my carvings are done in clay, and plaster (or cement) prior to pointing into wood.

eye) fill the view finder with the head and shoulders only. Take a number of shots (including the ones above) all around the head. I use Kodak TRI X black and white film, with exposure set at 200 instead of 400 the film calls for. This will result in good reference material. Colour film can also be used.

Clay

Two kinds of clay are commonly used by sculptors, oil or water-based. Oil-based clay is good for small figures and heads, and can be modelled directly from the 1lb block without having to use an armature. I would urge you instead to try the water-based clay, a 25lb bag will do. Any smooth stoneware type is good. You will need to construct a simple armature to hold up this clay while you work. (See the diagram.) Set the disk about 4" from the top of the post.

> ## 'When the idea of internal energy is revived, we will see a return to clay used as a transitional material.'

revived, we will see a return to clay used as a transitional material.

Most carvers have some idea in mind, and wish to carve this from a block (either solid or laminated). Drawing a front and side view and then bandsawing is Okay. However, even here many carvers do not have the drawing skills to do original work; I don't. My natural inclination is to think 3-dimensionally. My work is mainly portrait busts and figures, a demanding and exacting work.

Photographs

Photos of the chosen subjects are an important part of this process. Full frontal, profile and oblique views are necessary. Seat the subject in a swivel chair — close to a north window, on a sunny day. A dark background is useful. A soft fill-in light or a reflecting sheet of white cardboard on the shadow side is also good. Now, using a tripod, with your camera set at eye level, (check by measuring from the floor to the

¼" plywood
8" dia. disc.

⁷⁄₁₆" holes

³⁄₈" dowell
shellac all parts

Plywood base
18" x 18" x ¾"

15"

1½" x 1½" pine

Head Armature for Clay

Just Kelly
Clay model

For this first session, we will build a ¾" or full-sized head. Tape a ¼" thick coil of newspaper around the post then construct an egg-shaped form from clay around this post.

We will be working down to the the chin only, for now. Using your frontal and profile photos, shape the clay to follow the outlines. At this stage, we want no details (no hair, no eyes, nose or ears).

Use a piece of 1" pine, shaped into a paddle to pat the clay with.

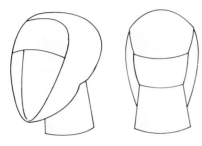

General Planing of the Head

Try to see the planes of the forehead and cheeks in the photos, and shape these into your clay. Make sure the post is set back from the front of the head or the slant of the neck will run into the post later on. Constantly refer to the photos and try to get the general shape.

Draw a line vertically up the centre of the head, then mark in the location of the eyebrows, end of the nose and centre of the mouth. Using your thumbs, scoop out eyesockets just below your

mark for eyebrows. The nose and mouth are mounds built up on the surface of your head shape. Check the nose; most beginners simply make a wedge shape but the nose spreads across the whole face.

After checking your profile photos to make sure the eye sockets are deep enough, build a mound in each eye. Then, using a pointed wooden modelling tool, incise into each mound the inside outline of the eyelids. The idea now is to create an eyeball inside these lids.

By the second or third session, you should drop the disk down about 5" or 6". Again tape with newspaper to the post and fill the space with clay for the neck area. You should also support the head with another pin while doing this, and remove this pin when the neck is complete. Modelling the ears, the hair and shoulders (if any) comes next. Check the outlines on your photos to build the hair and ears. When the bust is complete, lift the head – along with the disk – off the post. After drying for a day, turn head upside down and hollow it out using wire end tools. Your head should be about 1" thick all over.

My inclination is to take the modelling as far as I can in clay, and then go to the wood. You may not wish to complete the head in clay to that extent – but shape the proportions and expressions only. Either way is fine.

Water-based clay should be dampened by spraying with water while you work. This as well as

covering the clay with wet cloths and plastic bags between work sessions.

When your head is complete, armatures removed and sculpture hollowed out, put three plastic bags over it (one at a time) with twist ties. Remove one bag each week for three weeks. Clay shrinks about 15 per cent while drying and the idea is to dry it slowly to prevent cracking.

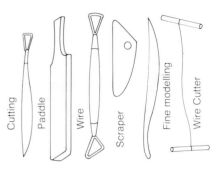

Basic Clay Tools

I urge you to borrow or purchase *Modelling a Likeness in Clay* by Daisy Grubbs, Watson Guptill Publications, 1515 Broadway, New York, NY10036. She describes a step-by-step approach to successfully completing a head in clay.

In the next article Joe describes the pointing system he uses to transfer the dimensions of the clay model to wood — a method stone carvers have used for centuries.

Just Kelly
Bleached mahogany

Prime-time
A self-portrait of my wife and me. Near life-size, walnut. Won Best of Show at the two principal wood carving shows in North America in 1988 — the Canadian National Exhibition and the American Wood Carvers Congress

POINTING

TECHNIQUE

Joe Dampf

A measured approach to carving

Joe Dampf is one of Canada's finest and best known woodcarvers. He begins each carving by working out proportions and other details with a clay model.

Joe conducts classes and seminars in both Canada and the USA as well as maintaining a studio in Don Mills, Ontario, Canada.

It is possible to duplicate your modelled head in wood by simply measuring and using calipers. But it's much more accurate to use a pointing system.

As mentioned in my first article, 'pointing off' is an ancient sculptor's method of transferring measurements from either small or full-scale models, into stone (usually marble). I will now outline a simplified pointing method which can be used with wet or dry clay models, and plaster or cement castings. There are many books

rectangular pieces of ¾" 20mm plywood, cut slightly larger than the outside dimensions of the clay model. Lightly nail these together, then cut them out on the table saw and sand the edges using a sanding disc on the same saw.

Fasten your dry clay model to the centre of one of these plywood squares, by tacking down 1" 25mm square pine strips, about 1" 25mm away from the base of the clay model. This will result in a recess or channel into which you will drive a number of nails part way into the plywood base. These nails

block so that the glue lines do not run down the centre of the face but rather across, from ear to ear, a less critical area. Temporarily nail this block to the base, turn it over and drill countersunk holes for 2" 50mm number 12 wood-screws. I use seven to 12 screws depending on the size of the block.

To rough out the block, line up the plywood bases on your bench top with the model in front of the block. Next, by sighting from the front, draw with a crayon a line about ¾" 20mm away from the model, a slightly oversize head shape. I then use a small electric chain saw to make horizontal cuts up to this line, about 1" 25mm apart. Chisel these away and then repeat the process for the side views. I use a piece of heavy chipboard 30" x 60" x 1¼" 760mm x 1525mm x 32mm thick with a melamine surface on all sides to work on. Clamp this onto your work bench so that it projects out into the room. Then take the wood block and drill holes in each corner of the plywood base right through the chipboard worktop. Bolt securely. You are now able to reach all four sides of the carving and sit right up to it. Place your clay on this same surface.

Before refining the headshape, I point, carve and mark with Xs all the high points on the wood, using the model as a guide. You will end up with X's on all the high points of the face, nose, eyes, chin, etc., on both the model and the carving. These marks will be about 1" 25mm apart on delicate areas and 2" 50mm or more apart on the broader areas.

Pointer System

My pointer system has two arms. I use a machinist's surface gauge. These are available from tool supply houses for about $35.00. The arm on the upright is for transferring the X points from clay to wood. The L-shaped arm on the base of the pointer indicates the distance from the edge of the plywood square to the

Just Kelley. Bleached mahogany. ¾" lifesize. Showing pointing system

which describe the casting technique but, for less complicated single heads or figures, dry clay models work quite well. Dry clay is fragile but with reasonable care will easily stand up to this measured approach to carving.

To provide reference surfaces for the pointer, we need two

will anchor the liquid plaster with which you will fill the trough.

The carving block is then attached to the centre of the second plywood rectangle. To do this, line up the two bases on your table and then, by moving the block around, align it with the model. You should also orient the

YOUR WAY

pointer base. This L-shaped arm does not come with the gauge. I made it from a used car aerial.

Raise the two pins slightly above the block. Next cut the sleeve of the aerial a little longer than the outside measurement of the pins. Then solder the sleeve to the tops of the pins, making a solid unit which can be lifted out at will. Bend the end of the arm into a right angle about 2″ 50mm long. Before returning the arm to the sleeve, get a couple of ½″ 12mm, hard rubber discs from your local plumbing supply. Drill holes in the discs for a tight adjustable fit. The discs are then pushed onto the arm, either side of the pins, next to the sleeve.

It is also possible to have this arm made by a machinist or tool and die maker. One of my students made one for me. It has a knurled wheel for tightening and is easier to use than the aerial.

Transferring

To transfer the X points, set the pointer base up against the plywood base under the clay piece, adjust and tighten the L-shaped rod and move and tighten the upper arm until it just touches the clay. Mark this spot with an X using a felt-tipped pen or marker. Next, move the pointer over to the plywood square under the carving block. The L-rod locates the base in the same place along the plywood. You can tell from the distance between the pointer base and the carving block how much wood needs to come off. Carve this wood away until the pointer touches in the same place as the clay and mark with an X, using a pencil.

This rough carving is done with a ¾″ 20mm or 1″ 25mm No 8 gouge. Cut across the grain whenever possible for maximum control. When you are within ¼″ 6mm of the desired depth, use a ½″ 12mm No 9 shallow-end spoon gouge. Cutting across the grain, take out a scoop to the final depth, and locate the X in the

Tree of Life

Made from ¼ of a very large walnut stump turned upside down. The piece shows the ultimate use of the pointing system as a pointer was used to make sure the clay sculpture fitted the wood. In other words, the shape of the wood dictated the composition. The 13 figures were modelled in clay separately then moved around to relate to one another

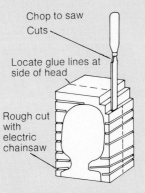

Chop to saw
Cuts

Locate glue lines at side of head

Rough cut with electric chainsaw

Orient block to have enough wood

Sight from wood block to clay. Draw rough outline 1″ oversize on wood

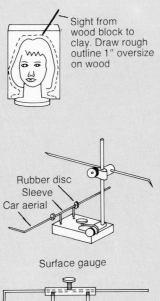

Rubber disc
Sleeve
Car aerial

Surface gauge

Machinist-made L-shaped arm

bottom of the scoop. Repeat this process over the entire head, from the high points to the low, using all four sides of the plywood bases for reference.

The next step is to connect the X points, by shaving wood from X to X with shallow gouges, all the while observing closely the contours between the X's on your clay piece as a guide. You may wish to practise this technique prior to committing yourself to the large block. Sharp tools and proper tool selection is important.

The final shaping is done with riffler files. I often use rat tail files, machinist needle, and other small files which I convert into rifflers. Heat the ends with a propane torch, red hot, bend to desired shape, reheat red hot, and then plunge into water to harden.

I never use sandpaper to finish with. I prefer heavy duty Scotchbrite pads, 3M COARSE BROWN No 7440. You can cut these into 1″ 25mm or smaller discs and use them on a flexible shaft power tool. The discs must be used with care, especially with soft woods, but will result in a smooth sculpted look. You will be pleased with the way these discs wear, as they soon assume the shape you are working on and will continue to cut until worn down.

Finishing

Finish the carving by completely sealing the surface with any clear flat finish, rubbed down with fine

Scotchbrite. I use a brush then a small cotton cloth pad and rub in this finish in a few coats. The pad will remove the excess and prevent surface build-up.

If the colour of the carving is uneven due to defects, or if the wood grain is too pronounced, use a matching stain, after sealing the wood. I like to use Varathane gelled wood stains from Flecto Co. These stains will intermix to get the desired shade. Cover the entire surface with a thin coat and then, using a soft cloth, wipe it all off. Some will remain on the wood. If this seems too dark, thin with a solvent prior to application. You may have to do this more than once. If there are areas that still show, add thinned stain with a small brush. When completed, you should end up, not with a heavy stained look, but rather a thin glaze of colour. Final step is to cover the whole piece with a coat of clear flat finish using an aerosol spray so as not to disturb the stain.

I will be the first to admit that clay modelling and wood pointing is not for everyone.

There is much to be said for direct carving, and I occasionally use this method. But for me the place to be immediate and daring is not in unforgiving wood but rather in soft, easily worked clay. I believe anyone who wishes to do original work must get away from using two dimensional patterns and force themselves to think in the round, by avoiding the block and bandsaw approach to carving. ■

ALL THAT GLITTERS

JEREMY WILLIAMS DESCRIBES HOW TO MAKE A PAIR OF MATCHING GILDED PANELS

One of the interesting things about commission work is sometimes it involves carving something a little out of the ordinary. One such job was to carve and gild a pair of matching oval panels. That type of work does not come along every day.

While much of the carving was straightforward, a number of points arose which may be of interest if you are thinking about producing panels with mirror images, or gilding a design.

I wrote an article on how to carve a pierced panel in issue 8 of **Woodcarving** but for those who missed it, here are some general details about pierced carving.

DRAWING MATCHED DESIGNS

As the design of one panel was a mirror image of the other, only one drawing was needed. I did it with felt-tip pens onto layout paper, because this grade of paper is thin enough to give an imprint of the image on the reverse.

The carbon imprint is over-drawn with felt tip, negative areas hatched in and saw holes drilled

This provides a mirror copy. As is generally the case with working plans, you should avoid any detail too tiny to be carved with the tools you have.

The panels were to be positioned close to glazed doors which had bamboo leaf patterns. So the design had to be made up of leaves which would complement those on the doors.

It can be quite exacting to draw an oval and it usually involves using a trammel to plot the shape. (I have covered the technique in detail in my book, *Decorative Woodcarving*, published by the Guild of Master Craftsman Publications).

Another way, if the size does not have to be exact, is to seek out a picture framer and cadge or buy an oval picture mount of an appropriate size and draw round it.

The important shape is the oval for the outer edge. The inner edge of the border can always be drafted by hand and trued up later.

Next, I had to plan how the panels would be fixed. I opted for key-plates. Positioned on either side of the border at the widest point, they would help to check any subsequent movement of the wood.

WOOD SELECTION

At 400 x 295mm, 15¾ x 11⅜in, the panels were a little under the size of A3 paper. The width meant searching for good quality boards of sufficient size. I preferred to work in lime (*Tilia vulgaris*) and was fortunate to find suitable timber at my local stockists, Colletts Woodworking of Mount Hawk, Truro. The boards were planed to a thickness of 20mm, ¾in. Any thicker and the panels would have looked too cumbersome.

It is normal to choose the side nearest the tree centre for the panel front

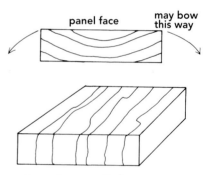

panel face   may bow this way

use quarter-sawn timber for greater stability

I put the design on to the wood with graphite coated carbon paper. At this stage, you usually have to select which face of the timber will become the panel front.

It is normal to use the side which was nearest the tree centre. The annual rings pointing upwards will tell you which side that was, when viewing the end-grain. Then any subsequent shift of the timber will cause the face to bow not cup. But for better stability, I chose to go for boards from close to the middle of the circumference (quarter-sawn), with the annual rings set nearly at right-angles.

When transferring the drawing to the wood, make sure you do not use it the same way round twice. If you don't check this point, you may well find the

Top **The negative areas are cut with a jigsaw**
Above **Trimming back to design**

Above **Preliminary shaping**

designs do not mirror each other when you have already started carving. So mark the design on one side 'Drawing 1' and on the other side 'Drawing 2'. When you use the drawing the second time, make sure the side labelled 'Drawing 2' is face up.

Another check you should carry out is to hatch all negative areas which need cutting away with felt-tip.

OVAL SHAPING

This stage involved shaping the wood to form matching oval outlines. First I cut each panel piece, slightly larger than the drawn oval. I used a bandsaw with a narrow blade.

The saw cuts were stopped short of the lines I had drawn. A V-tool cut line can be added as a safety measure,

if it is made just inside the waste area. Similarly, a vee line on the panel back, just in from the border, will stop splits and tears during sawing.

Then I butted the two panels together, back-to-back, prior to edge sanding. I stopped them slipping by holding them together with short panel-pins. The pins were driven a little way into a couple of negative zones of one panel, and the heads cut off.

I aligned the second panel and brought it down on top of the first with sufficient pressure for the cut pins to enter and hold. I find sanding is made easier if the designs face outwards. It also helps the alignment if you drill small holes through the negative zones, close to where the panel pins will go.

Removing the wood from the

negative areas is quite straightforward. I cut the larger part away with a jigsaw, and used a coping saw for the smaller gaps.

CARVING

I carved the design sequentially, with each part of the design, and its mirror image, being treated in turn. This was to ensure the symmetry of the design was maintained on each panel.

To aid this, I mounted the panels side-by-side on the bench. Then I could switch from one to the other at will. If I had carved the first panel completely before starting the second, there would have been noticeable discrepancies.

I prefer to hold my relief carvings in place with backing boards and strips of wood. This allows you to turn the carvings around as the work progresses.

I trimmed any remaining waste wood back to the design, using gouges where possible, for a clean-cut edge.

But it is not unusual to have to resort to rasps and rifflers in some parts. I incised overlapping areas of design with a V-tool for greater clarity when I started the modelling.

CONTOUR MODELLING

I modelled the contours of the leaves in two stages, interspersed with reducing excess wood from the back of the panels. This entailed giving the design some partial contours, then turning the panels over to work on their backs, before returning to the panel fronts to finalise the faces of the leaves.

It can become confusing, when working from one carving to the other, to tell which leaves have been worked over and finished, and which still need attention. I marked each pair off as I progressed.

I had to decide on the strength of the wood I needed to retain. Reducing the rear of the design area can be something of a balancing act. The aim is to give the impression of lightness and delicacy, while retaining sufficient inherent strength, especially where the design meets the border. Overlapping some of the leaves for greater thickness can be an advantage.

I also needed to decide on the degree of under-cutting. I had to take final viewing distance into account. The panels would be seen at close quarters, so a reasonable amount of under-cutting would be necessary, or the leaves would seem too heavy.

LEAF TEXTURE

I decided the texture cuts had to be applied boldly, or their effect would be negated by the thickness of the gilding. Bamboo leaves have surface ridges which give a corrugated look. The carved leaves were stylised. Some were texture cut with a small No.7 gouge, others with a No. 10 and parts toned down by sanding with crumpled 500 grit paper. I brushed the sanding dust clear afterwards.

Many people are put off gilding. They think it is highly complex, entailing the use of archaic substances such as earth pigments, rabbit skin glue and expensive gold leaf. But this is not the case.

Top **Modelling the leaves**
Centre **Crumpled paper is used for sanding**
Above **Applying Fontenay Base**
Above right **Gilded panel**

coating, it does provide an under-tone for the gilding varnish. There are various shades available, depending on the required type of final finish. My panels needed to be bright gilt. Liberon recommended Chantilly gilt over a yellowish shade of Fontenay Base.

I painted the base-coat on to the wood. The greater the care taken at this stage, the better the final finish will be. I applied four coats of Fontenay Base, each being allowed to dry and then thoroughly rubbed down with fine grit paper to remove any blemishes. I found a brass suede-shoe brush useful for smoothing back the textured parts, whereas sandpaper would have worn the cut edges too much.

A skew-shaped switch type brush with soft bristles was ideal for painting both the Fontenay base and the gilt varnish. I gave the panels even coats of gilt, but I could have achieved an 'aged' look by letting some of the base show through in places.

This type of gilding is very effective and brings added dimension to your carving with very little hassle. ●

Jeremy Williams started carving at the age of 14. He has extensive experience as a teacher, and runs his own courses on woodcarving. He contributes to several woodworking magazines and has also written a book, *Decorative Woodcarving*, published by GMC Publications.

The process can be accomplished without too much difficulty if you use ready-made materials. Good preparation of the wood is vital to success. I opted to use ready-made Fontenay Base and gilt varnish, both supplied by Liberon Waxes.

GILDING

Fontenay Base has the consistency of single cream. It seals the wood and, like the gesso used with gold leaf, masks the grain of the wood. Although it is not possible to build up a thick

CABIN CRAFT

ANDREW PETERS EXPLAINS HOW HE DESIGNED AND CARVED A SERIES OF SEASCAPE PANELS FOR A YACHT

Maritima is a company which creates hand-carved work for yachts. We research period styles, traditional designs for restoration projects and design work for today's yachts in classical and contemporary forms.

This commission started some time ago, when I was asked to submit designs to carve 38ft, 11.6m of woodcarving panels for the interior of a 164ft, 50m yacht under construction in Holland. The work was to be in the form of 13 relief carved panels to run across the top of shelves, over doorways, in alcoves and so on.

They ranged in length from 18in, 46cm up to 5ft, 1.5m. A theme was chosen of the seven seas, with the carvings being installed into seven different areas of the yacht. Each area was to have panels depicting scenes with fish, birds, shells, and stars which were distinctive to each ocean.

Andrew Winch Designs were the interior yacht designers. I worked with them to become aware of their concept for the yacht, the decorative style and the sort of atmosphere it would create.

The use to which a room is put naturally has its affect on the atmosphere, together with the choice of furnishings and lighting. The carving should encompass this, enhancing the space and retain a unity with the other decorative features within the rooms.

DESIGN CONCEPT

The designers produced some excellent artists' impressions of each area which helped me to visualise the space, distance and angles from which the carvings would be viewed.

The scale of detail within the carving was established from this, together with the idea of having an underlying pattern. This would be visible from a distance, and create a pleasing effect in its own right, but also draw the observer nearer to see the detail. The patterns would reflect something of the spirit of each ocean, so this decided which ocean should be in which room.

The Arctic was placed with the cool marble of the bathroom. In the guest hall where the carvings were near to the observer, more emphasis was placed on bigger detail than the overall pattern, with some striking shapes which could be recognised as you walked past.

The height of the carvings above floor level was established to ensure the perspective would be right, and the position of the lighting, which was to be low voltage down lighters placed above and in front of the panels, was noted for its affect on relief.

....

Panels after gilding

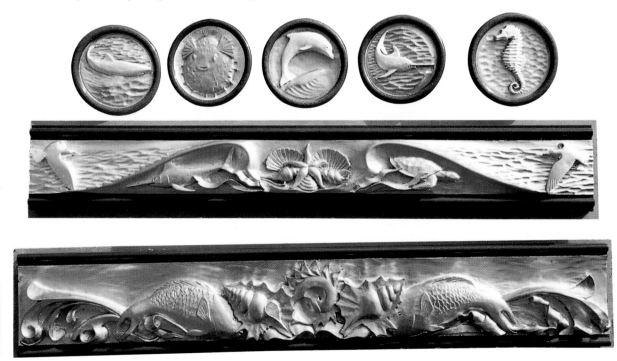

GILDED PANELS

I produced a sample panel which was taken to the boat and found to work well, but then the client decided he would like all the carvings gilded. The sample was carved with a deep relief and lots of undercuts. This is not the easiest thing to gild, especially in Brazilian mahogany (*Swietenia macrophylla*), as its fairly open grain would show through the gold.

Gilding also dramatically alters the affect of light and shade by reflecting light into areas which were previously in shadow. This called for a re-think in the designs, assessing what affect reflected light would have. We carved areas so light was either reflected away from areas that needed to be in shadow, or took advantage of the gold to highlight areas, by reflecting light into them.

One panel, for instance, had an albatross soaring high above the sea. If we had left bare wood with the light source from above, the bird would have created a large area of shadow on the sea. By tilting the surfaces of the carving, the finished gold surface reflected light onto the area giving a more realistic effect.

Left **A banquet of shellfish marked out on the mahogany panel**
Below **The carved banquet before gilding**
Bottom **Undercutting the wood**

NATURE STUDY

Next came a period of research, which started at the Natural History Museum, to see which specific breeds of birds, fish, and types of shells were to be found in each ocean. An underlying pattern emerged for each panel expressing the spirit of the sea. Often the shape also gave a clue about its location, with the detail being made up of the life that lived within it.

To give some contrast to the gold, the gilding was designed in gold and silver, which also helped to make the underlying pattern more discernable. In the Antarctic ocean, we designed two birds, their wing tips scribing a shallow curve to denote the bottom curve of the earth, which also divided sky from sea and contrasted in gold and silver.

The dining room in the yacht had a shallow domed ceiling with the night sky over Singapore. It seemed fitting for the panel in this room to depict the Indian ocean and at over 5ft, 1.5m in length, there was room to express the richness of the area.

The panel started at the Cape of Good Hope with an anchor and African shell and stretched to the Sea of Japan shown with a Japanese Wonder Shell. A horizontal line running equidistant through the panel, signified the equator and acted as a still point where the eyes could rest amid the activity in the foreground.

Here the waves rose and fell to show fish and a turtle, or rose up to form crashing waves. This, in turn, all formed part of the underlying pattern of seven waves along the equator.

Tropical birds were to fly towards the centre piece of the panel which showed the fruits of the sea offered up in a banquet of clams, oysters, mussels, seaweed, lobster and a string of silver pearls. Colouring the calm sea behind the waves with silver helped to define the equator and also gave the thin panel a better depth of field.

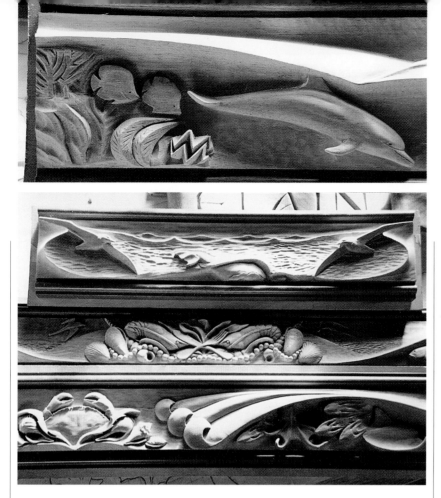

Above **Dolphin and fish panel showing the reflection of light**
Left **Part of the finished banquet panel before gilding**

CAREFUL CARVING

Ten months later with the designs approved, a large crate arrived at the workshop from Holland containing all the timber. Each piece was machined to it's finished size, with an edge moulding polished to match the surrounding timber of each cabin.

The central part was left blank for me to carve, with approximately 1¼in, 32mm carving depth. There was certainly no room for mistakes, carving right up to a polished wood edge.

As with all my work, the carving was carried out completely by hand, using mainly old tools collected over the years from antique tool dealers, and many hours looking through junk shops for the once treasured tools of past craftsmen.

They seem to hold their edge so much better, and the individual shape and age of the handles has the distinct advantage of enabling you to instantly recognise the chisel needed next. Staring at a set of identical handles, examining the sharp end of the one you want, can waste so much time and interrupt the flow of the work.

It was useful to work up a panel to a good stage of completion and then leave it to work on the next one. It's surprising what the eye will see after a day or two when you view the work afresh, with still enough wood to make adjustments.

CONSTANT CHECKS

I constantly checked the perspective and relief effects by placing them on a shelf which had been fixed at the right height and with the correct lighting to match their final position in the yacht. On tricky areas of relief, I placed a piece of silver foil to see the affect of reflected light.

While working, I prefer to listen to the sound of the chisel than the radio or commentary in the head, and find it's only when there is this total connection with the senses, that the work flows and has life to it. This is part of the beauty of work produced by hand.

After nearly 500 hours of carving, the panels were ready to be gilded. To stop the grain showing through the gold, the carvings were prepared with gesso. This is a thick material, which obliterates the grain, along with a lot of fine detail, but it can be smoothed and recarved to bring detail back.

It was a lengthy process, but the result was a surface which gave the gold it's brilliance. The gold chosen was 23ct Italian, supplied loose leaf and fixed with a 24hr size. The silver was fixed with a 12hr size, with the gesso coats coloured to suit the two materials.

The hardest discipline was probably to stop at each point when I instinctively knew it was complete and not to listen to the little voice which said, "Just take off a bit more here", or "add a bit more detail there", which invariably ruins the purity of a design or adds too much to an already completed effect.

Finally the work was repacked into its crate and sent on its way to Holland for fitting. I had a strange mixture of feelings as I swept up the last few woodchips in the now empty workshop.

There was a touch of melancholy as an enjoyable project came to an end, but also the satisfaction of it having reached completion, to be enjoyed by others hopefully for many years to come. With lots of new ideas from what I had learned, I went on to the next project. ●

Andrew Peters trained in carpentry and joinery and furniture restoration. He is a self-taught woodcarver but has had some tuition in drawing and sculpture. A life-long interest in yachts, classic boats and wooden boat construction led to the formation of Maritima in 1991. The company aims to design woodcarvings to complement today's innovative yacht design.

You can contact Maritima for commissions at 76 Mathews Way, Stroud, Gloucestershire GL5 4EB. Tel: 0836 323431

MASTER CLASSES

IAN FORD DESCRIBES HIS FIRST WORK IN BUTTERNUT, CARVED WITH A LITTLE HELP FROM THE EXPERTS

I have long been an admirer of carvings by Fred Cogelow. Fred has won major awards in the USA and Canada, written books on woodcarving and designed his own unique range of skew gouges. Most of his work is executed in butternut (American white walnut, *Juglans cinera*). So I was anxious to obtain some and try it out myself.

However, when I went to California on holiday, despite visits to timberyards and talking to a number of carvers, I was unable to obtain any. Fortunately, Fred was planning a visit to the UK, and kindly agreed to bring me a suitable piece of wood, about 11 x 5 x 5in, 280 x 125 x 125mm.

FOLLOWING STYLE

To me, butternut and Fred are synonymous, and being very much · influenced by him I decided that the proposed carving should reflect his style. I quickly settled on the idea of an old woman's head, which while relatively simple would have the complication of including glasses.

I'd produced a carving with glasses before and had attempted to carve them from the same block. After much fussing I swore (quite literally) never to carve glasses in situ again, but to make them separately and fix to the head afterwards. But when talking to Fred it was obvious that making something a little more difficult was no reason not to do it, if the carving would be more aesthetically pleasing. So, he said, what was I whingeing about! With knuckles rapped, I therefore set down to carving.

FAST WORK

To the purists among you, my apologies, for there was no drawing or modelling before carefully proceeding to the wood. I just fixed it to the clamp and roughed it out. From the first few cuts I could tell this wood was going to be a pleasure to work with. It has a distinctive pleasant smell and cuts quickly, easily and cleanly. Without the use of power tools and after only a couple of hours' work the carving had proceeded to quite an advanced stage.

Next some of the details were defined, including cutting in the neck and collar. The bow at the front was left deliberately large, to be tackled at a later stage. The glasses remained ominously filled, but at some stage they would have to be hollowed out and the correct position for the eyes established. This was the bit I wasn't looking forward to but, as the textbooks say, the carving should be worked as a complete entity. I also wanted to get at least the basics of the piece there so I could get Fred's views on it before he went back home.

WORDS OF WISDOM

Unfortunately I wasn't around for Fred's departure and so left the partially completed carving and a note asking for some pointers. I received a sheet of paper with arrows on. Shame the man's sense of humour doesn't match his carving ability!

However, he was good enough to add a few words, which others might find helpful. First he noted that it was easy to see I was an accountant, as I obviously didn't want to waste any wood. But he pointed out that if I had made the head smaller it would have given more scope for shoulders and thereby broken down the cube-like nature of the carving. The face was still too square generally and the neck needed further recessing. He also marked the areas which needed greater depth, principally around the mouth and nose.

His other major point was the unnatural symmetry; he suggested tilting the glasses and base to break down the rigid straight lines. The eye needed closing and tilting down and he thought I'd been a bit premature in undercutting the glasses. That apart, it was a nice piece of wood.

ACTING ON ADVICE

Concentrating on the points raised by Fred, I put in another four hours' work. The neck was recessed further and the collar and bow taken down and back. The other eye was also cut in, and I put in some work on the ears and hair, to get them to a similar level of completion as the rest of the carving. At this stage another critique by Fred would have been useful, but with him a few thousand miles away this wasn't possible, so it was a case of reviewing

OVERLEAF

Top left **Butternut is so easy to carve that after only a couple of hours' work, and without using power tools, the piece was already taking shape**

Top right **At this stage, leading carver Fred Cogelow gave his comments on how the work could be improved, making it less square and rigid**

Bottom left **Bearing Fred's comments in mind, another four hours' work brought the carving to this stage**

Bottom right **Further helpful comments were made at this stage by another professional carver, Ray Gonzalez**

the photos I was using as a rough guide, and bearing in mind the points raised earlier.

There then followed a first tidy up over the whole carving. As the wood

A large hole in the rear of the block meant that it was simpler to let the wood dictate the shape of the lower half

was carving so well, I decided on a tooled finish although I did sand the glasses, more for contrast than any other reason.

I also started to remove all the waste from under the collar. I hoped this would break into the cube-like nature of the carving – which Fred had been critical of, and doubted that I could rectify. I allowed the shape of the supporting piece, other than the bow, to be dictated by the wood, as at the rear of the block was a largish hole running diagonally through it.

FURTHER GUIDANCE

At this stage I was fortunate to get some guidance from Ray Gonzalez, another renowned professional carver, though this time from the UK. The main points Ray felt needed correcting were that the brows were too square and needed rounding; the cheekbones should be a little more prominent; the eyes needed tilting a little more; the chin thinning down and the neck

recessing still further. Unfortunately the nose was too long but it was too late to rectify this.

Again these comments were taken on board. Ray pointed out that many of these faults were common to most amateur carvers. Perhaps he was trying to make me feel better.

AND FINALLY

After this stage, progress – which had been slow – came to a grinding halt, with work commitments mounting up and the need to finish another carving, a gift. So it was a number of weeks later that I returned to the carving and decided it was time to attack the back and hollow out 'Gran', as I now thought of her.

Having drilled the pupils and nostrils straight back into the block to

give me a rough guide, I started hollowing out the back using my newly acquired Pfingst flexible shaft machine and assorted burrs. This took several hours. It was then a case of a final tidying up, including the hair and its texturing.

A base was obviously required: I used 2in, 50mm thick applewood boards, settling on a circular base with a tooled finish that would look more 'friendly' and in keeping with the carving than a formal square one. The base was sealed and waxed, but the carving was just oiled with thinned-down tung oil. That's how Fred finishes his carvings – and if it's good enough for him...

So that was it, my first carving in butternut, but hopefully not my last. My recommendation to fellow carvers is to get hold of some of this wood and try it for yourself. ●

Ian Ford works for the AA as a management accountant. He started carving 12 years ago, with Welsh lovespoons, and has since progressed to carving people, particularly heads and masks. He is heavily influenced by Fred Cogelow and the American style in general. (Photograph courtesy of the Basingstoke Gazette)

PROJECT

SHORTCUT TO SHORTBREAD

A CHANCE DISCOVERY WHILE LAYING SOME CARPET SET JOHN RAWLINGS ON THE TRAIL TO CARVING HIS OWN BISCUIT MOULD

I must have been on my knees for about half and hour before I spotted the biscuit mould. I was helping my brother to lay carpet in an empty flat and the new owners had already started moving some of their things in.

I was in the kitchen making some tea, when I saw a wooden biscuit mould hanging on the wall. It was about 254mm x 200mm, 10 x 8in, made of a light coloured, unfinished wood. The carved details were crudely cut into the surface. It seemed very quickly made with none of the detail fussed over.

I had read somewhere in a book on treen, that wooden food moulds

The original photograph.

have been made for hundreds of years, mainly in Holland and Belgium, to many different designs, some of animals or famous people of the day, even of well known buildings, and of course domestic scenes.

I was returning the next day so I decided to photograph the mould so I could make a tracing and eventually a copy.

The next day was sunny so I was able to lay the mould on the floor and photograph it using black and white film. The strong directional light from the window helped to pick out detail in the mould.

I made the print in my own makeshift darkroom to more or less the same size as the original, and took a tracing from that to copy onto the wood in the time honoured fashion.

EXERCISE

I would not be using the finished piece as a food mould, but it would be a good exercise in carving and I did not anticipate it taking a great deal of time.

There was not much information in my local library on the subject of moulds or the carving of them, only that food or biscuit moulds consisted of a flat piece of wood of manageable proportions with a design cut into the surface to form a pattern or picture in mirror image form, so when the mixture was pressed into it and turned out, the result could be baked in the oven.

CUTTING

The general outline of all the main parts, the clock, stove, bird and cage, were copied onto

the block. I used oak (*Quercus robur*) with the grain running from corner to corner. This didn't matter much, but I had to be careful at times as I progressed.

Lime, (*Tilia vulgaris*) would be an easier wood to carve, but the grain in oak adds to the finished piece. Of course oak cannot be used with food because it contains tannin. Biscuit moulds are usually made from sycamore (*Acas pseudoplatanus*), which has no flavour.

THE CLOCK

The clock was cut in using a No 3 gouge and skew chisel for the straight runs. The top half of the clock was cut to a depth of 6mm, ¼in and the bottom half slightly less, say 3mm, ⅛in, and the actual dial 8mm, ⁵⁄₁₆in, I drew around a coin for this.

A No 6 gouge was used for some of the tighter curves, and a small chamfer cut in the uppermost part of the clock.

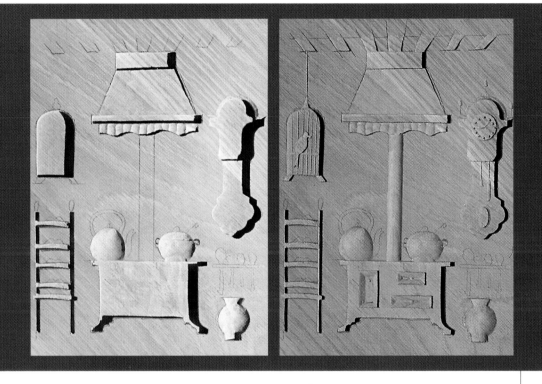

The biscuit mould gains detail in stages.

The top part of the cooker hood was a straightforward exercise in cutting in with a straight or skew chisel, that is stabbing down vertically, then easing out to the required depth of 3mm, ⅛in. The stove feet were cut in the same way but were more awkward, and a small 2mm, ⁵⁄₆₄in No 3 gouge was used here to get in tight.

The outline of the bird cage was also cut in to a depth of 3mm, ⅛in using the skew chisel, and a No 8 gouge for the curved, top part of the cage. The cut out parts of all these shapes could be scraped or sanded flat ready to take further detail.

The chair at bottom left was cut in with a straight or skew chisel and cut out with a 2mm, ⁵⁄₆₄in No 3 gouge to a depth of 3mm, ⅛in.

The two pots and the kettle on the stove were hollowed out with a 5mm, ³⁄₁₆in No 8 gouge, cutting down into the wood and easing out at the centre to a depth of 3mm, ⅛in.

COOKER

The middle section of the cooker hood, where the vase of flowers sits, was cut vertically along both edges to define the sides and then this area was lifted out with a flat chisel, cutting from the bottom and ending at the top, getting slightly deeper as the chisel progressed.

The bottom edge of the frill on the bottom of the cooker hood, was cut in using a shallow gouge to a depth of 2mm, ⁵⁄₆₄in. A mallet was needed here as well. The gouge was held vertically to cut through the wood fibres, reversing to produce a wavy line.

I then sliced gradually down to the bottom edge of the frill starting from the top, with a 10mm, ⅜in No 8 gouge on a slight angle, getting deeper as the gouge moved forward. This was repeated all along the frill to the ends. Some tidying up with a craft knife was needed in the corners.

The clock face, as mentioned earlier, was cut deeper than the rest of the clock after drawing around a coin.

The clock number positions were marked with a small punch, and the hands cut with a V-tool.

The three finials on top of the clock were cut with a small No 10 gouge, eased in at the top slightly and getting deeper as it progressed, and cut across at the bottom end with a craft knife. The V-tool was used again to join this part to the top of the clock.

The bars on the bird cage were cut with a small V-tool or craft knife, and the line suspending the cage was cut in the same way. The bird was cut with a 2mm, ⁵⁄₆₄in No 3 gouge and hollowed out.

The doors to the stove were pencilled in, a large rectangle for the outside edge and a small one for the inside edge. A straight chisel was used to join the two up by cutting downwards from the inside line to the outside line.

The flue to the stove was made with a series of cuts with a 10mm, ⅜in No 10 gouge cutting deeper and deeper until a sort of semi-circle was

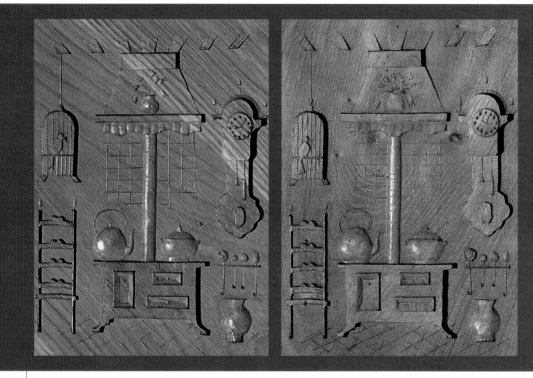

Far left **The finished mould.**
Left **The same mould made in elm (Ulmus procera).**

cut into the wood along the whole length, from the stove to the cooker hood.

The seven ceiling joists were cut in with a craft knife to a depth of 2mm, ⁵⁄₆₄in at the deepest point, and breaking out into the cooker hood. They were cleaned out with a 5mm, ³⁄₁₆in No 3 gouge gradually sloping back to the surface.

THE TULIPS

The tulips were made using a 4mm, ⁵⁄₃₂in No 10 gouge and a small V-tool, or craft knife. Starting at the flower base, the gouge held upright, was pushed down and levelled out as it reached the end of the cut.

The gouge was then pulled out without breaking the fibres. The mould was turned upside down and the three petals on each flower were cut out with the knife or V-tool.

The spoons or ladles were cut with a 4mm, ⁵⁄₃₂in No 10 gouge, stabbing down and levelling out to form the

bowl shape. The handles were cut with a V-tool.

The floor and wall tiling was made by cutting the surface very lightly with a small V-tool.

The chair, as described earlier, was cut with a 2mm, ⁵⁄₆₄in No 3 gouge and the scallops in the chair back were cut using a 4mm, ⁵⁄₃₂in No 10 gouge, stabbing down into the grain to the required depth, then breaking out into the chair back.

The tops of the chair back were cut in a similar way as the finials on the clock, with a small gouge. The clock pendulum was made with a small gouge, as was the kettle on the stove.

The whole thing was sanded to remove all the remaining pencil marks and any odd wood fibres cleaned up with a craft knife.

I gave the mould two coats of Danish oil to accentuate the grain.

The black and white photograph shows the original from which mine was copied. ●

John Rawlings is 47. He is a self-employed carpenter, working mainly on the renovation and restoration of older buildings around Bath, where he lives. He was interested in woodcarving for some years, but never found the time to make anything until he saw a course with Dennis Gilbert advertised at Charlton's Timbers of Radstock.

When the recession in the building trade came in the early 90s, he was without work for two years, but converted his back shed into a carving shop and was able to give more time over to carving. Back in full-time work now, he still carves at weekends.

A GNOME FOR YOUR HOME

ROGER SCHROEDER DISCOVERS HOW JOEL HULL CARVED A SCANDINAVIAN FOLKLORE CHARACTER

"When I carve a small figure, I'm in business with just a few tools," says Joel Hull of Port Jefferson, New York, USA. This retired physics teacher says most carving articles he reads offer a 'laundry list' of tools. "Some of these carvers probably tackle a small piece like mine with at least 6 or 7 tools, including a 9in, 230mm long chisel. This is overkill. I'm ready with three tools at hand."

The finished Norwegian gnome

....

Hull's style of carving, which allows for so few tools, is called flat-plane carving. Common among many Scandinavian carvers, this style is best described as flattening areas with knife cuts, hence making planes, and using a knife to remove V shaped wedges of wood.

Importantly, he does not use

sandpaper. Hull lists sanding among the 'S words' which should be shunned by flat-plane carvers. When planes are created, they come together as ridges or below-the-surface wedges and are left that way. An illusion of roundness or depression is created.

Plane carving has been popularised by carvers such as American Harley Refsal. Having studied this carving style in Scandinavia, Refsal has taught classes in the USA and Europe. Hull has been among Refsal's students.

TOOL ECONOMY

With only three tools, two of them knives, Hull is ready to carve a folk figure. The knife which removes the bulk of the wood is a Swedish Mora knife. With as much blade as handle, the tools offer a durable blade of laminated steel.

Hull says the Swedish knife may offer more of a blade than a beginner would be comfortable with. An alternative, which is his second-most used tool, is a knife with a short, interchangeable blade. The Warren knife is sold as a set of blades with a walnut (*Juglans spp*) handle and brass ferrule. This knife offers shorter blades than the Swedish knife yet has quality steel that keeps a keen edge.

The third tool in Hull's arsenal is not a carving knife but a Speedball no.1 linoleum block tool. Hull uses this linoleum V-shaped cutter to make a shallow channel, much as a gouge does. He uses this tool for only limited operations, but the effect produces depressions rather than wedges.

SHARPER EDGE

Hull doesn't overlook the importance of sharpening. His choice for sharpening stones are a combination of diamond and ceramic surfaces.

"To say carving is 80 percent sharp knife is conservative," he says emphatically. " In the beginning I carved for a year and a half before I learned what a sharp knife was. Now I know, I can't go back to using a dull one."

Before he starts to carve with a tool like the Swedish knife, Hull alters the shape of the blade. He points out most blades, though wedge-shaped, have a secondary bevel which does the actual cutting. Hull removes that by grinding it away.

The reason is the second bevel means he has to use more force to carve away wood. He explains, " With a continuous wedge, I don't have to work as hard. But this is only true with basswood (American lime, *Tilia americana*). Harder woods do require the presence of the bevel."

LEVERAGE CUT

Hull says many carvers, when they see a line on the wood, jam the knife in and go perpendicular to the surface to make some cuts.

When he starts carving, his knife goes in at an angle to pop the wood out.

Hull says this is not unlike chip carving, which is a process of removing a series of chips to form an engraved design that goes below the surface of the wood. It originated in Europe and has been found decorating old Scandinavian utensils.

Much of Hull's carving is accomplished with what he calls the leverage cut. With the knife held in one hand, Hull uses the thumb of the opposite hand to push on the back of the blade. Not only is there a mechanical advantage created as the blade slices the wood, but there is also added control since both hands are involved. The result is a very clean cut according to Hull.

But there is more to the leverage cut than just pushing the blade into the wood. The blade must slice as it is being pushed. Hull positions the blade near its tip and, as he pushes it into the wood, works it toward the base of the blade as he finishes his cut. He describes this as a skewing or snow-ploughing motion.

"I watch carvers working too hard

who haven't mastered this. You have to make the tool work for you." Hull compares the finished effect of this kind of cut to a burnished finish which is smoother than a sanded surface.

PARING CUT

Another cut in Hull's repertoire, a paring cut, involves pulling the knife towards his thumb. This cut is used when the wood grain or the position of the cut does not warrant a leverage cut.

To avoid cutting flesh instead of wood, Hull wraps the vulnerable thumb with racketball tape, the green gauzy material used on the racket handle to prevent slippage. Leather thumb protectors slide around too much, he says.

The only other cut Hull uses, though infrequently, is a perpendicular stop cut. A stop cut establishes a wall of wood that sets up a boundary, so adjoining wood can be removed. This nearly always requires directing the tool's cutting edge perpendicular or straight down into the wood. Hull usually uses a stop cut to slightly undercut an area.

FOLK CHARACTER

Gnomes are elf-like creatures in popular folklore from a number of cultures, including Scandinavian ones. For this project Hull has chosen a Harley Refsal pattern of a gnome, also called a Nisse, complete with pointed hat and clog shoes. It takes about four hours to bandsaw, carve and paint the figure.

He chooses basswood because it feels good to carve. After cutting a piece with dimensions of 7 x 4 x 3in, 180 x 100 x 75mm, he uses front and side profile patterns made using a flexible

Above left **The cutout for the gnome looks like a puzzle**
Above **Hull uses patterns made from stencil plastic**

piece of transparent stencil plastic.

He draws parts of the anatomy, such as the arms, on the plastic and then cuts through, making a pencil channel. This allows Hull to lay the patterns on the wood cutout and easily locate the details.

Hull's approach to bandsawing is different from most other carvers. First he cuts out the side profile but does not discard the background or glue or nail it back in place as others would. Instead, he treats the block as if it was a jigsaw puzzle in three dimensions.

Keeping the side profile and background together, he turns it on its side and cuts around the front profile. When this puzzle is taken apart, he has a figure with front and side profiles done, but he also has four outlined pieces left. Instead of discarding them Hull turns them into Christmas ornaments, either doing some low relief carving on them, or flattening and painting them.

With his three cutting tools in front of him, Hull works quickly through the strategic cuts that will produce a flat-planed gnome. He starts with the ears where he makes stop cuts. These cuts not only help define the ears but also prevent them from being carved away as work is done on the face and hat.

After locating the ears with stop cuts, Hull works on the shoes. By turning the carving upside down, he can decide with simple pencil outlines

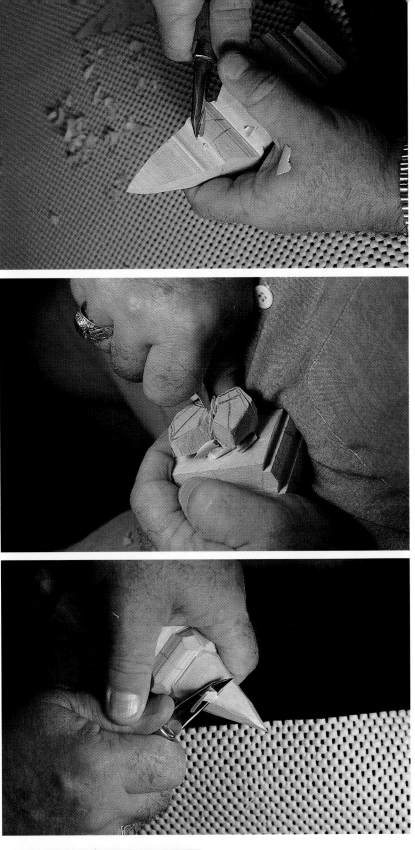

From top to bottom
● **Carving the ears with a Swedish knife. This is one of the few times he uses a perpendicular stop cut to establish anatomy**
● **Removing wood from the feet by cutting out wedges of wood. Notice the lines indicate how he has splayed the feet**
● **Rounding the hat with a series of flat planes which will not be sanded smooth. Hull pushes the blade with his thumb to make a leverage cut**

whether he wants the shoes to be splayed or kept parallel. Then he shapes them with a series of cuts which take out wedges of wood from between them and from their outer edges to give the illusion of roundness.

Then Hull moves on to the hat and coat. "When I see beginners start with a square block, they tend to leave it square, so rounding has to be done consciously," he observes. When working on the hat, he strives for an ice-cream cone shape as he removes wood.

He also takes time to undercut the hat by taking out wedges of wood where the forehead meets the hat. He says inexperienced carvers work on the face and worry about the separation of the hat later. This results in a hat that looks more like a tight-fitting beanie.

THE FACE
Next Hull establishes the position of the nose with the help of a centreline. He works on the base of the nose first. From there he makes J-shaped cuts to locate the positions of the beard lines. This delineates the separation of the cheeks and beard. To add the sideburns he makes stop cuts.

Hull begins the eye channels at the bridge of the nose. Removing wood from either side of the nose brings out the nose and establishes the puffy cheeks. Hull works on the nose while looking down from the top. This serves to remove just the right amount of wood

Left Hull uses a Warren knife to establish the nose, cheeks and sideburns

from either side. He then goes back to the tip of the nose to give it roundness.

The gnome has a combination moustache and beard. The more gnomes Hull has carved, the more pronounced he has made the moustache. To raise the moustache he lowers the background by carving away some of the beard.

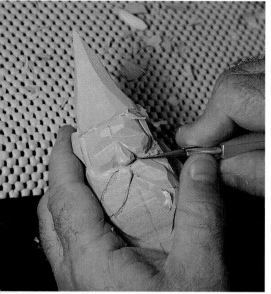

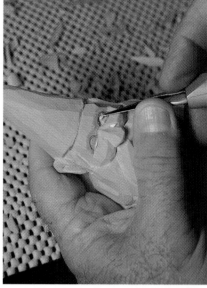

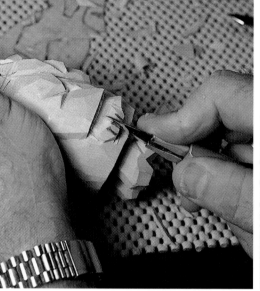

Far left **The eye channels are located by removing a few wedges of wood, the cheeks are defined and moustache is raised from the background**
Far left below **Hull works on the arms, fingers and thumbs**
Above left **To round the eyeballs, inverted pyramids are removed from each corner of the eye and then the eye is rounded at the top and bottom**
Left **The ears are defined by cutting out a question mark-shaped series of wedges**
Below **A linoleum tool is used to detail and separate the beard and moustache**

....

ears. He removes hard corners and makes what he describes as question marks inside the ears. This is done by taking out small wedges of wood.

The eyebrows are done with a series of wedge cuts made to suggest a sunburst pattern radiating from the base of the nose. Hull says because of the small size of these wedges, a razor blade or an X-acto knife with a No.11 blade can be used by those not as confident at working fine detail with a normal carving knife.

Next he defines and rounds the arms with a minimum of flat cuts. Finally he puts creases in the crooks of the elbows, one across each arm, and another 45° to that. Then he moves on to the hands, carving a thumb first and dividing the rest of the wood into four equally spaced fingers.

FEATURE DEFINITION

Hull has a formula for laying out eyes. Proportionately, he says, the width of an eye is one fifth of the width across the section of the head where the eyes are located, with one eye width between the eyes.

When he has located the eyes, he makes stop cuts in the corners of the eyes to create what he describes as inverted pyramids. Then he rounds the eyeballs with his short-bladed knife, so they are really rounded and bulging out.

Next he returns to working on the

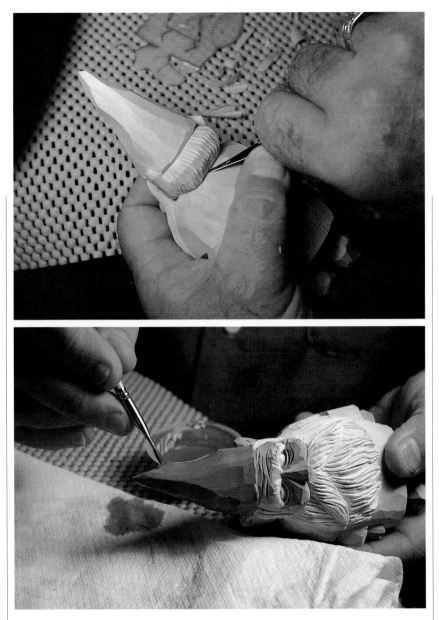

Left **He undercuts and separates the neck hair from the coat, which will help to keep the paint from running**
Below left **The paint is applied as washes, taking care not to flood the wood and minding gravity**

When the painted carving has been dried with a hair dryer, Hull dips the entire piece into a can of boiled linseed oil darkened with a walnut stain. "The painted gnome looks pale and washed out before dipping", Hull says. Finally, he lets the carving dry for at least a day.

Hull says a good carving can be ruined by a poor paint job. But he says you shouldn't be afraid to make mistakes. "Some of my better carvings have resulted from working out the mistakes I made. And if that didn't work, I had some unique kindling wood." ●

Roger Schroeder is a prolific writer and lecturer on woodworking, construction, sculpture and carving, as well as a cabinetmaker and amateur carver. He combines these activities with a full-time job as a high school English teacher, specialising in teaching creative writing and research.

The Warren Knife is available from Warren Tool Company, 2209-1 Rt.9G, Rhinebeck, NY 12572, USA.
A similar tool is available from Craft Supplies, The Mill, Millers Dale, Buxton, Derbyshire SK17 8SN.
Tel: 01298 871636
CeramCoat is available from Delta Technical Coatings, Whittier, CA 90601, USA.

The beard and moustache have to be defined with hair separations. Hull uses the linoleum tool to work from the bottom of the beard up to the tops of the sideburns and then down towards the shoes. He then turns the carving around and does the neck hair that protrudes from under the hat.

He finishes that area by taking out minute wedges of wood between the ends of the hair and coat, a technique that will later help with the painting.

PAINTING

Hull stains the wood using watered down acrylic paints. He prefers CeramCoat, a liquid which comes in two ounce bottles. Hull comments, "Acrylics dry quickly, and I can even speed up the drying with a hair dryer."

He points out watered-down paints tend to run, but the v-shaped wedges of undercut wood that separate various parts of the anatomy from the clothes help keep the paint from running into adjoining areas. It is as if he carves a barrier to stop the unwanted flow of paint. This gives a neat, precise appearance to the painted carving.

Hull uses two different brushes when painting. One is a ¼in, 6mm angle shader for applying the watery paints. Another, a spot brush, paints in the eyes using undiluted paint.

Hull has his favourite colours for painting his carvings. For the face and hands, he uses Fleshtone or AC Flesh. The hat is done with Tompte Red and the coat is in Christmas Green. He applies English Mustard to the shoes.

The beard, eyeballs and eyebrows get a heavy wash of Antique White and the irises are coloured with Wedgewood Blue. To add realism to the eyes, Hull applies a white dot at the two o'clock position with a round toothpick.

CHESS CHARMERS

JOHN MOON DESCRIBES HOW HE CARVED A CHESS SET BASED ON CHARACTERS FROM TOLKIEN'S LORD OF THE RINGS

I first became fascinated by chess and chess sets when at college. I remember seeing Ingmar Bergman's film *The Seventh Seal*, which centres around a chess game between a knight and Death, and being inspired by the chess set.

Further inspiration followed from a description of a mighty chess game, or battle, in J.R.R. Tolkien's *The Lord of the Rings*. I have made three sets based on descriptions of the characters, or pieces, in this book.

The first set, which was my first carving project, was cut with a bandsaw, chisels and knives from alder (*Alnus spp*), maple (*Acer spp*) and walnut (*Juglans spp*), but told no stories.

The second set, made about two years later, was made of basswood (*Tilia americana*), and involved the use of more sophisticated tools and techniques. This set was a vast improvement and attracted a lot of attention. At the time of writing it was on display at the Long Island Chess Museum, New York, who bought it.

My third set, again made from basswood, is the subject of this project. I first drew every character over and over again until I was satisfied with it. I then transferred each drawing to a block of basswood using carbon paper, and trimmed off excess on the bandsaw.

I left two or three 'arms' from one side to the edge of the block to stabilise the block when I turned it 90° for its second run through the bandsaw. Once done, I removed the arms.

CHARACTERS

Each character was first shaped using coarse Karbide Kutzalls cutters. Dust was blown away from me with a small fan so I didn't breathe it in. As I went over the wood the character gradually emerged. Small parts (ears, noses, fingers and toes) were rounded off to be finely carved later.

Above **Characters set on the board**
Left **Triangular sanding fingers and the jig used to make them**

Using chisels and knives I first did the flatter surfaces and then the outer edges of the ears, nose, fingers, toes, etc. The smaller they got, the easier they were to break. Knives and chisels took off the fuzz caused by the carbide cutters.

Next came the fine carving of eye sockets, nostrils, grooves in auricles, separations of fingers and toes, collars, edges along hems, etc. Tiny diamond-coated carving points, small scalpel blades, and many tiny, dental grinding bits were of great benefit here.

A hole for each solid brass escutcheon pin, to be used as a button, was drilled with a bit slightly narrower than the pin, but the pin was inserted later.

I fitted the glass eyes, then removed them and set them aside in small, individually labelled vessels. Glass eyes are made in pairs by dipping both ends of a wire into melted glass at the same time. If you lose or damage one eye, throw its mate away. If you try to mate unrelated eyes, your character will appear to have anisocoria (unequal pupils) and that is surprisingly easy to see. I obtain my glass eyes from Craftwoods in Timonium, MD, USA.

All swords, shields, axes, etc. had ⅛in, 3mm diameter hilts or handles, and the hands that held them had ⁹⁄₆₄in, 3.5mm diameter holes. This meant swords and shields could be exchanged.

For final sanding I went through the grades of sandpaper down to 320 grit or finer, using compressed air to blow out every groove and hole before advancing to the next grit.

SANDING JIG

I made a helpful jig which was simply a wooden table top insert made for my table saw. It was used to closely surround a saw blade which was tilted 7°. The tip of the blade just touched the side of the wooden fence at a height twice the thickness of the wood to be cut. I made a first cut from the edge of a board, turned it over end-to-end, made a second cut and repeated this over and over again. This allowed a relatively safe cutting of 14° isosceles triangle-shaped strips of wood around which I glued 1½–2in, 38–50mm strips of sandpaper using contact cement. When one strip wears out, I simply break it off or cut it off with my bandsaw between the adjacent strips of sandpaper. These sandpaper fingers fit most edges and grooves, and cost next to nothing to make.

Far left **The router jig for cutting out the castle decks**
Left **The bandsaw jig for cutting out the castle crenellations**

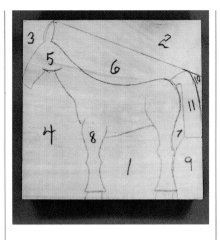

Above **Original drawing transferred to a block of wood**

Right from top to bottom
- **Sections 1–4 removed**
- **Sections 6–7 removed**
- **Sections 9–10 to be removed**
- **Final removal of sections 11, sides of the tail**

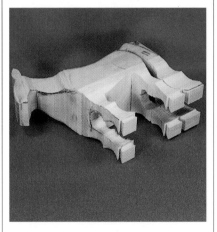

KNIGHTS AND HORSES

Cutting out the horses on the bandsaw was quite different from cutting out the characters. The cutting sequence is important and is shown in the photographs. With the horse lying on its side I cut away blocks 1–4, then turned the horse onto its back and cut out the sides of the head and neck (5). Then I turned the horse back onto its side and removed blocks 6 and 7. Next, with the horse on its tail I cut off the outer and inner sides of the legs (8). Then I laid the horse on its side and removed 9 and 10. Finally, I put it on its feet and trimmed down the sides of the tail. The grinding, carving, sanding and finishing were then quite straightforward.

Once a horse has been made, a knight must be matched to fit him. This matching curve was easily found by bending a ⅜ x ½₆in, 10 x 1mm strip of lead over the horse's back.

CASTLES

The black castles were easily formed with the bandsaw. The doors, windows, and edges of the bricks were then traced using a compass, ruler, straight edge, and a fine pencil. The windows and doors were traced first, then the horizontal grooves, and the vertical lines last. A sharp, pointed knife was used with a straight edge for initial cutting, followed by a small V-chisel.

I used a router table with a fence and stops on both sides of the bit to cut out the floor of the top deck. I used the bandsaw with a stop behind it to cut out the crenellations. I made a smooth floor for the deck with a square piece of ⅛in, 3mm birch (*Betula spp*) plywood.

The white castles were more complex and mainly turned on a lathe. I also used a drill press, a router with a fenced table and a jig, and a bandsaw with a jig.

The 'rule of chess' says the king is the tallest of all the characters, but a castle is not a character, so mine are all taller than their kings. And they look better.

So far I had spent at least a day and often longer on each character. Sanding was especially time-consuming but essential for good results.

GLASS EYES

After final sanding I drilled a tiny hole into the back of each eye socket into which I inserted about ⅝in, 15mm of the 'dipping wire' still attached to the back of the eye. This kept the eyes looking in the same direction. I put a bit of epoxy on the back of each eye and inserted it into its hole and socket.

Once the epoxy had dried I covered each glass eye with a thick coat of Luma Liquid Mask (made by Daler-Rowney, Bracknell, England). When dry, I could paint, stain and seal. When the finishes and sealers were all dried, this material was easily removed with a tooth pick, a pin and forceps, revealing bright, realistic eyes. Without the mask you could find each eye has a hazy cornea or cataract from the sealer tightly bonded to the glass.

FINISHING

I began finishing only after the last character had been sanded and blown clean of dust. Most of the wood was stained more than painted. The first task was mixing a lightly coloured oil base stain, often referred to as a wash. I added a small amount of Grumbacher oil paint (usually a raw sienna or a flesh-like colour) to 3 or 4 mls of boiled linseed oil and thoroughly mixed them. It should be no thicker than the linseed oil itself and should

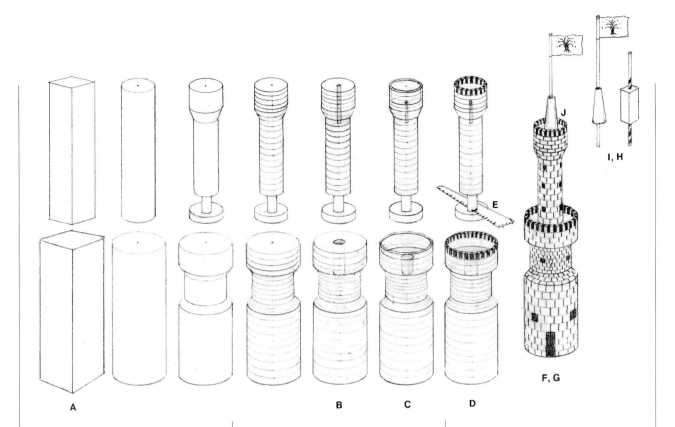

A   B   C   D   E   F, G   I, H   J

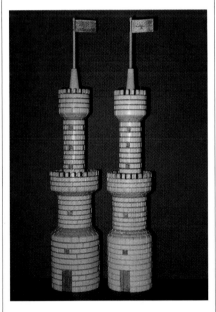

lightly stain but not opaquely paint the wood. The grain should remain visible.

I always test this with some similar scrap wood before applying it to a carving. I applied the wash coat generously and to all surfaces, allowed it to soak in and, after four or five minutes, carefully wiped off all unabsorbed stain, especially any in grooves, corners and holes. Each character was then stainable (or paintable) for the next four or five hours, but once it had dried, further colour applications were virtually impossible.

I added each succeeding colour,

Above **Fig 1. The sequence for making white castles. After rounding and shaping on a lathe, the horizontal grooves are cut with a skew. The tops of both sections are drilled, the decks cut out on the router jig, and the crenellations cut on the bandsaw jig. After the carving of the bricks and other features the two sections are glued together and the flagpole fitted loosely into the top hole**
Left **White Castles**

....

mixed as described above, to its intended site, applying the darkest and the thickest colours last. Though the colours don't run into adjacent ones they can run over them if too much is applied. Fine, careful painting and staining was needed using small (5-0, 4-0, 3-0 and 2-0) brushes.

As more surfaces were stained so the characters became more difficult to hold. I used a ⅛in, 3mm extra-long drill bit to make an obscure hole, usually between the legs, into which I temporarily inserted a ⅛in, 3mm dowel to serve as a handle for final painting and subsequent drying while avoiding accidental smearing of one colour over another.

A few days were needed for thinly coloured oil to dry thoroughly, but if a thick paint has been used, two or three weeks or more may be required before handling. Once all surfaces were

completely dried, I sprayed them several times with either a Grumbacher's Matte Fixative or a Krylon Crystal Clear Acrylic Spray Coating which has a bit more gloss.

ACCESSORIES

Finally it was time for swords, shields, helms, crowns, etc. In my preceding sets, such items were made of wood, and however I finished them, they still looked like wood. So I took a brief class on how to make silver jewellery using 'lost wax' casting.

Most people in the class were making a single item, usually a ring, but I continued my work at home and returned in a week with wax models for 28 items, including two crowns, three axes, three scimitars, three helms, 16 swords and one very large spider. These

Some of the silver castings

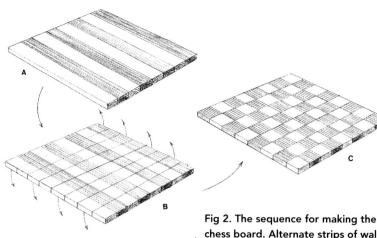

were each attached to one or two separate wax hubs using wax sprues, and the two sets were centred in iron reservoirs.

Each set was then covered with investment (while still a liquid), debubbled in a vacuum chamber, and allowed to harden. Once hardened they were placed in a furnace in which the wax disappeared. While still hot they were filled with melted sterling silver and spun in a centrifuge. They were cooled, and the solid castings were separated from their investments. I had never done this before and was fascinated by what emerged.

The castings were ground, filed and then polished using white diamond Tripoli, and finally a fine polishing material called Zam. The Tripoli and Zam were used with 3in, 75mm muslin and 3in, 75mm chamois wheel buffs, respectively (while wearing protective lenses). The resulting items were polished to such a shine I feared the importance of their owners might be lost, but that did not prove to be the case.

I made a set of helms, and once they had been ground and polished I noted that though they appeared to fit their owners satisfactorily, they often fell off if subjected to slight movement. Silver helms do not grip wooden heads at all well! It took a bit of trial and error to come to a satisfactory solution.

If I lined a helm with thin cloth material, such as silk or nylon, it still fell off with ease, but if I used thin, soft leather it fitted much better. Each of the four triangular openings in the helms were individually covered with slightly larger triangular pieces of soft leather.

These were glued to the inside surfaces of the silver helms. I used Super Jet, a medium viscosity cyanoacrylate adhesive, and applied it only to the silver. It solidifies in seconds. One tiny drop is all that is required for bonding a whole, triangular piece of leather. If a gluer is not careful he may unintentionally provide some of his own leather! Cyanoacrylate adhesive should be used with great care.

Although the use of soft leather enhanced the fitting of hats to heads I still was not satisfied. Finally, I took about a dozen 1in, 25mm x 18 brass escutcheon pins, ground their heads while spinning them in an electric drill, dipped them in silver flux, and bonded

them with a tiny bit of silver solder. Then I drilled tiny holes in the top of each helm along with tinier holes in the top of each head and, in effect, nailed helms to heads.

The white king and queen needed some gold, and I got professional help for this. Two silver crowns were chemically cleaned and then each, for about 30 seconds, was plated with pure, 24k gold using a (potentially lethal) cyanide based solution and an electric charging system. The results were lovely.

The Balrog needed horns, so I spent $1.25 on a tagua nut (often referred to as 'vegetarian ivory'). I flattened one side with a disk sander, and then carefully ran the nut through my bandsaw, cutting it into ⅜in, 10mm slices. From these I ground two horns and fitted them carefully onto the sides of his head. I snipped off the caps from a pair of 1in, 25mm x 18 brass escutcheon pins, sharpened them and inserted them into the bases of the new horns using a tiny drill bit and a dab of epoxy. Once dried I mounted the horns on the balrog, and he really became frightening and obnoxious.

I must admit to taking some liberties with the Lord of the Rings story and characters. I painted some brown rather than black, as black masks detail and makes characters featureless. I found it almost impossible to carve chain mail, and hobbits should be barefoot with hairy legs, but mine aren't.

CHESS BOARD

Chess boards can be made from many materials and in many sizes from miniature to over life size. The one I made for this set was walnut and maple, glued and biscuit jointed together. I started with a straight, flawless piece of each and planed them to ¾in, 20mm thickness.

I cut four strips of each wood and jointed them to make 3½ x 30in, 90 x 760mm. These were placed against one

Fig 2. The sequence for making the chess board. Alternate strips of walnut and maple are glued side to side. The second cuts are made and alternate rows rotated before the second gluings

another alternately with their grains all curving in the same direction. The eight boards were glued and jointed together using Titebond II and 56 No.20 biscuits, clamped and left to dry. The biscuits were placed every 3½in, 90mm between the rows.

When dry, I drew a large triangle in pencil across all eight strips so they could be reassembled when cut again. I trimmed one end straight and true and ran this edge against the table saw fence set 3½in, 90mm from a fine cross-cut saw blade. I cut all eight rows at 90° from the first set of cuttings and then loosely reassembled them.

Decide which way you want the grain to run (N–S or E–W). Get behind the edge of the board where you will be to play (white corner to the right). If the grain looks fine, turn over, end to end, rows 2, 4, 6 and 8, and you should have the chess board with the grains going in the right direction. The grains of adjacent rows now curve up/down in opposite directions, thus counteracting any tendency for the board to warp. If you want the grain running in the other direction simply turn the whole board over and rotate it 90°.

I did the second set of gluing with another 56 biscuits, clamped and left to dry. When sanding, a large professional 30in, 760mm belt sander was a great help. The board was finally fixed to a foundation block and finished. ●

John Moon was a paediatric physician and surgeon in Washington until he retired in 1987 to concentrate on his woodworking hobby. A prolific writer on medical matters in the 1960s and 70s, he has also written several articles for the American magazine *Fine Woodworking* over the last three years.

CARTOON CHARACTERS

JOHN MARSHALL EXPLAINS HOW HE TRANSFERS HIS DRAWINGS OF COMIC FIGURES TO WOOD

Baseball pitcher

When Canadian sculptor Christopher Rees introduced me to the basics of carving, he told me how to select tools and execute simple relief carvings on basswood (*Tilia americana*) slabs.

He coached me in the use of chisels, gouges, veiners and so on, impressing upon me the need to keep tools sharp. He claimed most accidents occurred when people used blunt tools, a fact I soon learned and was even quicker to remedy.

Having worked as an architect, and familiar with making casual flourishes with a pencil or brush on paper, the transition to using wood-cutting tools and wood was difficult to master. The skill of sharpening the tools was a great deal more demanding than sharpening pencils or cleaning brushes.

Even so, my drawing experience stood me in good stead and I soon realised how those lifetime skills would benefit me in this new field.

FUN FIGURES

Gradually my love of cartooning began to influence my work and I abandoned light relief, chip carving and traditional styles to concentrate on producing cartoons in the round, which I call my 'whittle people'.

This style of carving has become a focus of my recent work and I have produced figures in various humorous stances, attempting to capture the exaggerated expressions of golfers, hockey players, and other sportsmen, with an occasional dig at politicians.

I use a wide variety of knives in my work, but many other tools give me added versatility for shaping. As a non-traditionalist carver, I use whatever tool will give me results, ranging from bandsaws, scrollsaws, drills, chisels, rasps and rifflers to sandpaper. But knives play the most dominant role in the final process, so I have acquired a variety of knives for every conceivable situation.

I attribute my success to my

drawing talents, combined with a few aids I have developed to transfer my sketches from the paper to wood blanks. Most beginners are encouraged to develop their drawing skills to improve their chances of successful carving.

LAMINATED WOOD

Traditionally, woodcarvers execute their work from a single piece of wood, and would probably frown at any deviation from that procedure. I agree to some extent, where the finished carving is left unpainted.

My work is always painted, so I do not need to restrict the blank to one piece of wood and often add or laminate to achieve the shape and volume of wood necessary to accommodate the outline of the caricature. The grain and joints are covered with paint and the casual observer would not know more than one piece had been used.

Another advantage is I can select wood with the grain running in the direction of the arm or leg and avoid a potential weak spot where it joins the body. For instance, in joining an arm to the body, if the grain ran vertically through the blank, a weak spot may occur at the junction of the arm that projects from the body.

For extra safety, I reinforce joints by using a small dowel fixed with white wood glue. The results are dependable and strong. In most cases I carve heads separately and use a similar dowel or pin.

I use this method for several reasons. My style calls for the head to be on a larger scale than the body, so I may need a larger piece of wood than that used for the body.

The human face betrays the emotions and I find it more convenient to concentrate on developing the features to project the mood of the

This award winning pair of golfers is captioned "Blow or putt, it's still one stroke"

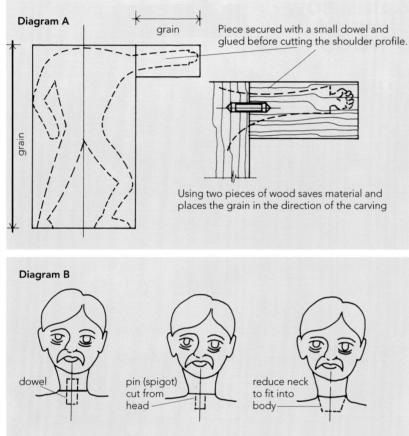

Diagram A

grain

grain

Piece secured with a small dowel and glued before cutting the shoulder profile.

Using two pieces of wood saves material and places the grain in the direction of the carving

Diagram B

dowel

pin (spigot) cut from head

reduce neck to fit into body

Three methods to secure a separately carved head to the body. A hole can be drilled in the body to suit the desired angle to set the head

way, I have tried to put my personal stamp on my whittle people.

Not everyone is interested in lampooning or exploiting the antics of sports characters, but my approach can be applied to your own selection of human or even animal subjects. Good targets are politicians and Disney-type animal characters.

SKETCHING PROCESS

Having selected a subject, sometimes by accidental observation of human behaviour, or by deliberate intent, I sketch the figure as I would approach a cartoon, but with one exception.

An artist can achieve a three-dimensional effect by the use of shadow for the suggestion of perspective. A cartoonist can exploit a situation by the clever manipulation of the pen and leaving the rest to your imagination. Even the impression of motion can be suggested by the addition of a line or two near or around the figure, but not touching it. Not so with carving.

Scottish golfer

caricature, without bothering about the body actions. Having achieved the desired results with the head, it is comparatively simple to set the most effective angle to the body and complete the portrayal of a specific activity.

There are several ways of securing the head to the body. Whichever method is used, sufficient wood should be left at the shoulders to permit final shaping around the neck and to avoid the head looking like a toffee apple on a stick.

COMIC EFFECT

Rather than using the formal method of carving human figures, where natural scale and proportion are needed to accurately reproduce the anatomy, my caricatures follow cartoonist's styles.

Heads are usually larger than normal, facial features such as noses, ears, teeth and chins are exaggerated, arms and legs are distorted, especially when the figure is shown in the throes of wielding a club, bat or stick. Other touches of humour are added when I want to draw particular attention to a characteristic feature.

The carving of a crooner illustrates the exaggerated scale of the figure's head and reinforces the reason for using a separate, large piece of wood. Artistic licence can be taken with the scale of hands, legs and feet, which adds to the comic effect.

Many different styles are adopted by cartoonists to create their unique caricatures and they become easily identified by those styles. In a similar

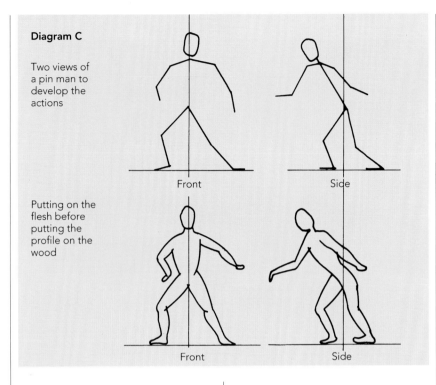

Diagram C

Two views of a pin man to develop the actions

Front   Side

Putting on the flesh before putting the profile on the wood

Front   Side

The three-dimensional effect can be achieved only by putting the right cuts on all sides of the blank and this requires imagination of the figure in the round. So I find it helpful to draw more than one view to guide the progress of the three-dimensional carving.

It is difficult for some people to imagine more than one view of a figure, especially when a complicated activity is being developed. So a series of sketches can help, making you aware of

details you would not otherwise see on the blind side of a photograph or one-dimensional drawing.

The number of sketches needed depends on the difficulty of the subject or the expertise of the carver, but it is easier to erase a pencil line than to remedy a mistake in wood. Don't experiment with a sharp tool when a pencil might solve the problem.

If you are just starting to carve small figures, it is a good idea to practice and experiment with pencil sketches to get the feel of creating different body movements or awkward stances, and to explore the effects of these positions before attempting the exaggeration of cartoon figures.

I take a few simple steps to prepare my sketch. First I draw a series of pin men to get the feel of the activity intended for the figure. Next, I fill in the body or put on the flesh, so I end

up with two, three or four views of my caricature.

I spend extra time developing the facial expression which is essential to the success of the figure. The mood or grimace must complement the figure's body language and I recommend experimenting with a variety of facial expressions, by making sketches portraying anger, fear, joy and so on and incorporating them into your own style of drawing.

There are many books available with illustration by artists and cartoonists which will guide you, but I urge you to develop your own style once you have mastered the rudiments of creating a smile, a sneer or a snarl on a face.

I spend time carving heads, experimenting with face shapes sporting beards, moustaches, bushy eyebrows, long hair or baldness, always attempting to create a new comic expression.

When I have completed the sketches, I transfer the drawing to the wood blank.

TRACING TIPS

Sometimes, the figure is relatively simple and I use a carbon paper over which I place the sketch, usually made on tracing paper. Following the drawing outline, I press through the paper to relay the picture to the wood. To avoid tearing the tracing paper and possibly the carbon paper too, I use a dried out ballpoint pen with a broad point.

However, when the figures become more complicated, I resort to another method which is useful if you are having problems controlling the

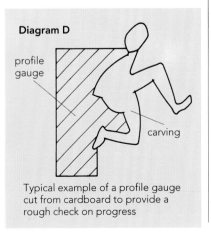

Diagram D

profile gauge

carving

Typical example of a profile gauge cut from cardboard to provide a rough check on progress

Fisherman in boat, entitled *Fishing For Words*

shapes when you have removed the initial cuts or obliterated the outlines from the blank.

I use a pattern which is actually a profile of the drawing transferred from the tracing paper to a thin, but fairly stiff, cardboard. I cut the board neatly with scissors or a knife to produce a facsimile of the sketch in a similar way a tool and die mechanic makes a profile gauge.

Then, using the pattern as a stencil, I mark the blank with the outline of the figure as a guide to cutting the wood on a bandsaw. As I make progressive cuts in the wood, many of the guidelines are lost. This is not a problem for the advanced carver, but it is for most beginners.

The profile pattern helps keep the picture available and be used as a check on the progress of your cuts by holding it in front of the work, as a silhouette of the figure appears. These patterns, when prepared for two or three views can make life easier. Another advantage is you can retain the patterns for repeat projects.

Control of shapes can be helped by cutting a pattern as a female gauge which is, in effect, a reverse profile of the finished carving. It can help to control the amount of wood being removed in case the eye waivers from the sketch.

ACHIEVING SYMMETRY

Although the intent to create comic faces involves exaggerated or distorted facial expressions, it is necessary to maintain a reasonable symmetry about the head.

Some people have difficulty balancing the features, such as ears and eyes. Because you are working on two different sides of the carving, there is a tendency to cut one ear too high, too low or too far back on the head. This might not be noticed until it is too late and you cannot make corrections without spoiling the desired effect.

In some cases, you might want to create a lop-sided face for comic exaggeration. However, some degree of balance and symmetry is necessary and knowledge of the proportions of the

human head can be helpful before attempting to exaggerating the features.

So some control is necessary, even for the cartoonist whose talent leans towards taking liberties with the main features of the face.

Starting with normal head and face outlines, I change those elements which will give me the most comic results to define the mood and expression, emphasising the key feature, such as the nose.

To ensure the ears do not drift from the normal alignment, even if they have been targeted for comic shaping, I resort to a simple profile gauge. The gauge marks the shape and distance on the blank and acts as a check to the cutting as work proceeds.

A larger, separate piece of wood was used for the head of the crooner at the microphone

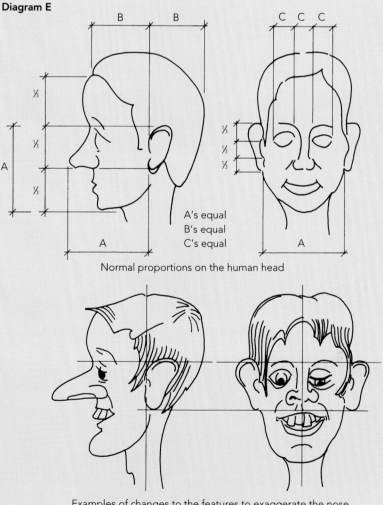

Diagram E

A's equal
B's equal
C's equal

Normal proportions on the human head

Examples of changes to the features to exaggerate the nose, ears, and teeth, but maintaining the symmetry of the head

Diagram F

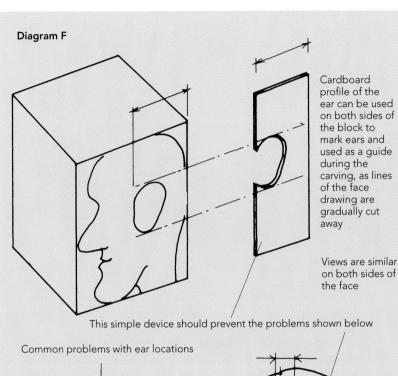

Cardboard profile of the ear can be used on both sides of the block to mark ears and used as a guide during the carving, as lines of the face drawing are gradually cut away

Views are similar on both sides of the face

This simple device should prevent the problems shown below

Common problems with ear locations

Front View

The ears are not level

Side View

left ear

right ear

The ears are not equidistant from the tip of the nose

Frustrated golfer

Since the wood is painted, there is no reason to use exotic or expensive woods, as it would be a shame to cover beautiful grains. I use basswood, butternut (*Juglans cinera*) or even pine (*Pinus spp*), but the latter has to be selected, fine grain and free of knots of blemishes. ●

As a young man John Marshall had a flare for drawing and painting, with an ambition to be a cartoonist. Fate decided otherwise, and he trained in architecture before serving in the RAF as a navigator in World War Two. He spent some time in Canada as a flying instructor, where he met and married Mary. He returned to Canada after the war and since retiring from architecture in 1983, has applied his cartooning talent to woodcarving. His 'whittle folk' have won him ribbons and awards and consist mainly of caricatures of sports people.

I paint my caricatures with acrylic water soluble paints and take the opportunity to enhance the impression of the mood. For instance, I give an angry flush to the face of a man with a temper or white hair to denote age.

ANCHORAGE

Because some of my whittle people are perched on one foot or appear to be leaping from the ground, I ensure adequate support from the base by drilling the foot or limb to receive a dowel or fine screw from beneath the base.

If I use a screw, I take care to avoid splitting the carving. Combined with white glue, the screw only needs to be tightened enough to ensure good adhesion of the two surfaces.

In most cases, my caricatures are anchored to a base with white glue, but additional precautions include miniature dowels or screws. One exception is when the caricature is on ice skates, when I resort to cutting small grooves in the base to receive the bottom of the skate blades. When glued, the results are amazingly strong and withstand most reasonable handling.

PUPPET LOVE

KEN FARRELL DESCRIBES HOW HE CARVED A LITTLE GIRL HOLDING A MR PUNCH PUPPET

I have a 40in, 1015mm high Pinocchio which stands in front of my glove puppet booth. I carved him from English oak (*Quercus robur*) and he is constructed to enable his head and waist to turn through 360°. His head and arms also swivel.

He's proven so popular I decided to carve a real child. My four-year-old granddaughter Laura provided me with the dimensions.

I placed a puppet on the figure's right hand for several reasons. The overriding one was it would be a greater challenge. My confidence still outweighed my ability but I felt the gap was closing.

I chose limewood (*Tilia vulgaris*) for particular reasons. It is reasonably lightweight and the carving would involve much handling. It's nice to carve, and I thought an oil paint finish would camouflage the butt joints. Also the grain isn't worth a second glance.

I bought three 8ft x 18in x 2½in, 2.4m x 460mm x 63mm slabs from Duffields sawmill at Melmerby North Yorkshire. They were quite flawed, knotty and distorted.

First I reduced them to 4ft x 9in, 1.2m x 230mm wide, then passed them through a planer leaving them little more than 2in, 50mm thick. I bonded nine full lengths of 4ft x 9in x 2in, 1.2m x 230mm x 50mm together using Cascamite, clamping them with 9mm studding and sash cramps.

The finished carving of Laura and Punch.

Above **The raw materials, the block of lime and Ken's granddaughter Laura.**
Below left **Additional pieces of wood were bonded to the original block to accommodate Mr Punch and Laura's hand.**
Below right **Bosting in with a chainsaw and axe.**

ROUGHING OUT

Later I bonded additional pieces of varying sizes to accommodate Mr Punch, and also Laura's hand. Armed with photos, drawings and measurements I drew the profile with timber crayons, which incidentally are identical to children's crayons. This wasn't performed as an exact science. It was etched in yellow, and when it looked alright I over-lined it in black.

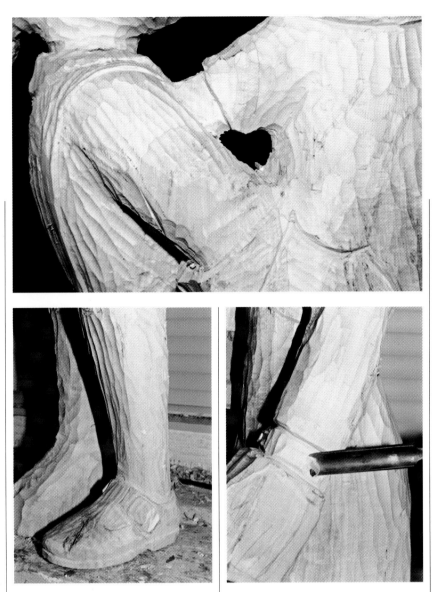

The subject is roughed out.

The method I used was little different from making a small mantlepiece carving. The tools, however, were more suited to removing a greater volume of waste. I used a 12in, 305mm Black and Decker electric chainsaw coupled with an Estwing hand axe to cleave off sizable pieces to retain for future projects.

At my first place of employment with the Forestry Commission, all the forest workers were craftsmen with hand tools. On occasions they would compete to see who, with seven pound felling axes, could splice the most matchsticks consecutively or strike a match by removing the least amount of tip. After five years I was able to compete in their games.

My American Estwing is made from super steel and is a valued tool in my workshop. Less so on this project where two 1½in, 38mm gouges featured in the initial carving, a No 3 and 5. The mallet I used with these gouges was home-made by merely

shaping a handle at one end of a boxwood log (*Buxus sempervirens*). I also used an Arbortech, another useful tool especially where end grain or knots/burrs are involved.

After I rolled the subject around many times between using crayons and gouges and standing it upright almost as many, I achieved a roughed out figure. What I missed with this carving was not being able to keep my eye on it, until I had produced a mountain of woodchips.

CARVING STAGES

From this stage the largest gouge I used was a 1in, 25mm No 5. From here on it ceased to be one large carving and became a series of separate projects. To gain maximum space to carve the child's head I carved the puppet's head.

The pictures show the complexities of 'fitting' a glove puppet and to balance the carving so the puppet looks right in relationship to the length of Laura's upper arm.

Top **Fitting the glove puppet to Laura's arm.**
Above left **Detail of the leg and knotty shoe.**
Above **Carving the blouse and skirt.**

Next, I had a bash at the legs. The left foot was 1in, 25mm further forward than the right foot, so first come first served. I became so absorbed in fitting a knotty shoe, I only came back to earth with my wife's voice asking me if I knew what time it was. I bet we're all asked that one!

The next day I 'crossed' legs. I inverted the toes as on the left foot, but while the left leg was bent at the knee, the right leg was locked. The weight was on the outside of the foot, raising the inner arch off the floor.

Let's take the shoe as an example to explain how I achieved each stage. I knew the predetermined length and width of the shoe, so I removed the excess. I also knew how thick the shoe

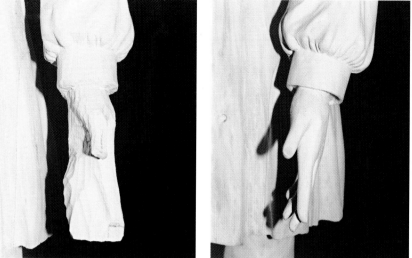

needed to be, so I removed the excess. Then I rounded it off leaving room for the buckle.

Providing you take into account the shoe's position in relation to the leg it will look alright. The next step was to see if I could weave cotton with these gouges. The cuff of the blouse was as good a place to start as any. I then put some folds in the skirt before moving on to the head.

HEAD FIRST

This was my first attempt at a life-size head so I modelled a clay one. I went astray with the head but feel consoled that I've learned enough to get it right next time. Access was difficult. That's not an excuse, it's a fact.

The left ear was pithy centre wood, which didn't want to stand up to the chisel. I advise you to take particular care when confronted with crumbly wood. A butt joint can be seen running through the eye and corner of the mouth. This was the dead centre of the jointed timber, the edges were at the front and back.

She turned slightly at the waist and head and I wanted her expression

Above and right **Laura's hand roughed out and finished.**

and movements to look like a young girl handling a glove puppet for the first time. Children concentrate so fully on operating a puppet they forget what the rest of their body is doing.

Three vulnerable extremities remained. As the pony tail was the least likely to damage I did that one first. The next project was Laura's hand. I wanted to avoid major errors at this stage so I dug out the Plasticine and made a scale model hand. This took about four cans of Guinness .

Mr Punch's free hand was the final act, again hampered by being unable to rotate the entire figure. I included several links between Laura and Punch. They both turned their heads and eyes to look at each other. Punch had a tassel, while Laura had a pony tail. Punch sported a ruff, Laura a fringed collar. Both had expressive hands and were pigeon-toed.

Below **Part carved head with clay maquette.**

Right **The carving before mounting and painting.**

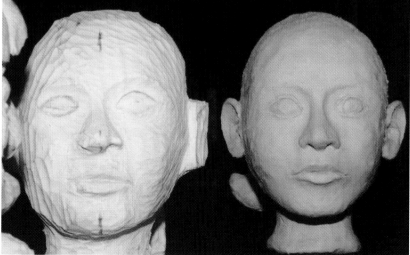

THE MOUNT

I chose to make the mount from burr elm (*Ulmus spp.*). I shaped a 14in, 355mm diameter circle using a chainsaw. It seems wasteful but I don't have a bandsaw. I hand carved four ¾in, 20mm dowels and jointed them, one entering each ankle and one entering each bridge of the foot.

My links with trees sometimes means I'm first in the queue for timber and I gained my tree from a nearby churchyard. I recall admiring the specimen when it lived. I wasn't in mourning for long when it caught Dutch Elm Disease.

I cannot tell the difference between

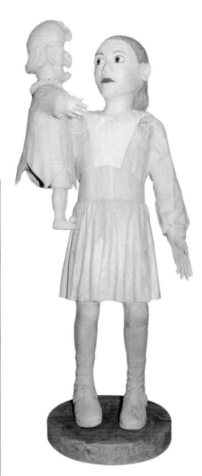

The painting process.

seasoned or deadwood if it is taken shortly after death. Many moons ago trees were seasoned still standing, by rounding them up with axes in preparation for felling, including chopping through the cambium layer to prevent sap flow. When they were dead they were felled.

PAINTING

Many people have told me over the years that woodcarvings must look like woodcarvings, and they must all be dark brown. This line of thought never influenced me. Surely the purpose of carving wood is to make it appear like something else and the closer to the real thing the better?

I used Winsor and Newton artists' oil paints carried in linseed oil, an ideal preservative for wood. I have hardly had any experience with this medium so I did feel inadequate at this stage. Before using oil paints again I intend researching techniques. The base was painted with four coats of clear acrylic gloss varnish. The project took three months to complete using all of my available time. ●

The finished carving of Laura and Punch.

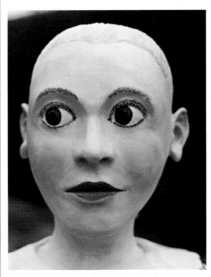

Detail of Laura's finished head.

Ken Farrell is the Punch and Judy man from Newton Aycliffe. He has enjoyed a lifetime's involvement with woodcarving, and although he does not claim to be an artist he is eager to share his passion for wood with anyone who will listen. Between puppet shows he demonstrates traditional puppet making and encourages those interested to buy a knife, an oilstone and *Woodcarving* magazine! If you want Ken as an attraction at your event, he can be phoned on 01325 317569.

Duffields Timber,
Green Lane, Melmerby, Rippon,
North Yorkshire HG4 5JB.
Tel: 01765 640564.
Black and Decker are at
210 Bath Road, Slough,
Berkshire SL1 3YD.
Tel: 01753 511234.
Estwing hand axes available from
King & Co, 182/190 Northgate,
Darlington DL1 1QY.
Tel: 01325 380808.
Arbortech available from
BriMarc Associates, 8 Ladbroke Park,
Millers Road, Warwick CV34 5AE.
Tel: 01926 493389.
Winsor & Newton art supplies
shop is at 51–2 Rathbone Place,
London W1P 1AB.
Tel: 0171 636 4231.

● COPY CAT

RAY WINDER DESCRIBES HOW HE CARVED A REPLICA JAGUAR XJ220 SPORTS CAR

In early 1992 I approached Jaguar Sport Ltd. and asked if I could photograph their £400,000 plus XJ220 supercar to help me carve a scale model. A reply came back that they had no objections and a meeting at the factory in Oxfordshire was arranged.

The problem with the real car is that photographs do not do it justice. It is much larger, meatier and more aggressive looking when you stand next to it. Yet this two seater (more like two leather armchairs actually) high-tech monster is capable of breakneck acceleration and a top speed of over 212 mph. The car really is quite stunning, a beautiful curvaceous piece of mobile sculpture. Little did I know at that time what a challenge I was setting myself.

CARVING TO SCALE

They were very helpful at Jaguar Sport and even brought a car outside so I could take elevational photographs (front, back, sides, etc) and close-ups of details. When the car was styled, a full size clay model had been made and then scanned so that all the information was contained on a computer. This meant that scale drawings could not be supplied and no computer print-outs were available, so I, and all the toy car makers, had to work from our own measurements and photographs. Having decided to make the model sixth scale, which would made the finished car around 32in, 815mm long, I prepared my own plans.

I decided that the wood had to be

Early stage after
rough shaping with
Arbortech disc

Elevated view of
the finished car

English walnut (*Juglans regia*) as this, in veneer form, has long been the traditional material for dashboards, door cappings and other details in the finest cars. The size of the block I started with was just over 32in, 815mm long, 14in, 355mm wide and 8in, 200mm thick. It was quite unseasoned, having been cut straight from a large butt.

Although most of the carving was technically not very difficult, the hardest part proved to be interpreting the actual shape and flow of all those subtle curves from photographs. Nice glossy paintwork might be very attractive but the reflections can give the eye distorted information regarding actual shape.

ACHIEVING SYMMETRY

Using my own drawings as a guide, the planned outline was bandsawn as accurately as I was able to at that stage, allowing extra wood around the areas that might need adjustment as the bodywork of the car progressed. I saw no point in trying to carve the wheels from the block, so these were turned and added later. I used an Arbortech cutter to remove a large amount of the waste wood. I also carefully drilled the underside of the car with lots of 30mm, 11/8in diameter holes to

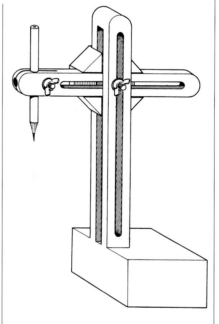

varying depths to help the drying and relieve any stresses. I now had to find a way to transfer measurements from my drawings accurately to the wood and, having carved one side of the car, to match the other side perfectly.

The traditional method of pointing seemed the obvious solution. I made a simple pointing device from scraps of wood. Two slotted vertical pieces of wood were attached to a heavy base,

another slotted piece was in turn attached to these with a wing nut at a 90° angle. This piece could then be moved both up and down vertically and across horizontally. An adjustable pencil was fixed to this for spanning curves and marking.

The side elevation drawing of the car proved most useful for transferring measurements to the wood. In order to do this I drew vertical parallel lines 20mm, ¾in apart over the top of the drawing. The rough block of walnut was then fixed to a base board which was also marked with lines 20mm, ¾in apart. By numbering the lines on the drawing and the lines on the base board, I was able to take a measurement from the drawing with callipers, transfer this to the pointing device and then offer this to the wood.

As I worked my way along slowly, I was left with a series of pencil marks on the wood which could be 'joined' up by removing the higher areas between. Although quite accurate, this only worked well for the outline and other obvious body details. All the curves and bulges had to be calculated by studying lots of photographs and then were transferred by eye to wood. This, as I said earlier, proved to be really rather difficult. One curve tended to dictate the line of another and if one area was not right, it didn't flow through to the next, and the shape was lost. It was slow work.

When I had eventually worked one side to a shape I was happy with, I then had to copy this on the other. This was where the pointing system came into its own. By gradually working around and across the car, essential measurements were taken and marked on the opposite side. With the car body roughly symmetrical, more adjusting was necessary to get the shape as near perfect as possible. I should point out that the carving of the

Top **The walnut block roughed out and fixed to the base board**
Above **A simple pointing device designed by Ray Winder**

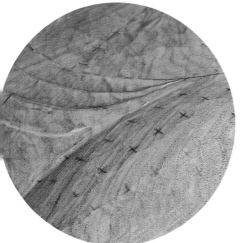

file. The wheels were turned on a lathe, requiring just a small amount of carving before I dowelled them into place.

Although I wanted the model to be reasonably accurate I was more concerned with portraying the overall flowing shape than making it a perfect scale model. However, I did feel it needed the wing mirrors and the windscreen wipers to complete it and so these were added later.

CONCLUDING THOUGHTS

This really did turn out to be a rather demanding project. It would have been much easier if I'd had a real car sitting outside to constantly refer to and measure, but that of course was not possible!

I realised that to copy something really accurately, especially when you are changing the scale dramatically, is more difficult than carving something of your own creation where you have the freedom to change the shape and accommodate any improvements or errors of judgement.

Despite all the care taken, when I finally placed my model next to the real car, I noticed that a few small improvements could be made. Jaguar Sport, however thought it the best model of the XJ220 that they had seen, so I decided not to be too hard on myself! The carved car is now in the private collection of a prominent member of a Royal family in the Far East, who owns several Jaguar XJ220's. ●

It was also difficult to find photographic reference of the venturi 'tunnels' underneath the car. None of the small scale plastic or metal models of the XJ220 were accurate enough to rely on for reference and I decided it would be better to ignore them than to inadvertently amplify their errors.

The finish on this carving needed to be flawless without a single ripple. Considerable time was spent getting rid of every scratch, progressing through various grits of abrasive and finally finishing with 1,000 grit wet and dry paper. The lines of the doors, windows, headlight covers etc. were scored with a scalpel and then further emphasised with a shaped riffler

Jaguar took place over nearly eighteen months, during which time I moved house, spent a lot of time renovating said house, and squeezed in paying jobs. If nothing else, this gave the wood a chance to dry slowly.

DUPLICATING DETAIL

There were some particularly tricky areas, like undercutting the rear aerofoil, which just required patience.

Top **Rear wing showing measurements transferred from other side**
Above **The front wing with pointing marks**
Right **Rear view showing detail and symmetry**

PROBLEMS AND HOW TO AVOID THEM

ROD NAYLOR LOOKS AT COMMON PROBLEMS IN ASSEMBLING AND FINISHING CARVINGS, AND SHOWS HOW TO AVOID THE PITFALLS

As a professional carver and restorer of wooden items, I am often amazed by the high quality of many carvings demonstrated these days. However, I am sometimes horrified by the lack of technical knowledge and understanding revealed by some of the techniques I see used.

I suspect some of the masterpieces I see will have a greatly reduced lifespan because of this lack of understanding, rather like those who took up smoking before they understood the consequences.

SHRINKAGE AND WARPING

Some carvers' habits which concern me are those which reveal a lack of understanding of how wood shrinks and warps. Some joints are doomed to certain failure.

When a log dries it loses around 25% of its weight, and it shrinks. The shrinkage is greatest around its circumference, much less across its width, and hardly noticeable along its length. With this knowledge we can calculate how a piece of wood will warp or split as water dries out from, or soaks into it.

Alignment of grain is important when jointing up a carving block. Any piece of wood containing the first annual ring, that is the heartwood round the pith, is most prone to splitting. But just to be awkward, woodworm prefer the outermost layers of wood, the sapwood just below the bark, which is usually paler and softer.

When jointing planks you should ideally use quarter-sawn wood where the annual rings run straight across, at right angles to the broad surfaces.

....

Left **A split in a tea caddy made from padauk heartwood.**
Below **Splits caused by drying round the circumference of a log. Warpage and distortion can also occur if drying is not controlled.**

Below **End view of joints in a carving block.**

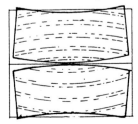

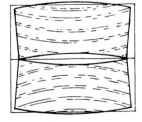

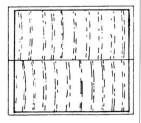

Wrong, shrinkage causes the blocks to pull apart

Better, but again shrinkage causes a gap in the joint

Best, quarter sawn wood is more stable

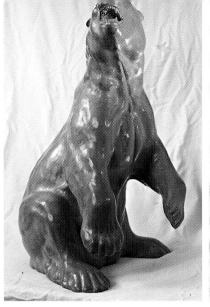

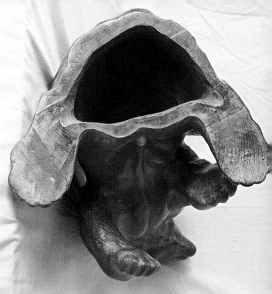

Problems arise when pieces of wood are joined to make a carving, such as wings to a bird or arms to a figure, where the grain is running in different directions. Frames for mirrors or pictures are invariably made in this way.

The separate parts shrink in different directions and this eventually results in ugly cracks.

SPLITTING

Splitting is also caused by too rapid drying of the wood. Keeping the wood in a plastic bag to slow down drying will often eliminate this.

If splits should appear, do not put filler in immediately, as this will eventually create even more stress.

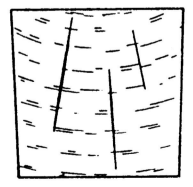

Top **Frames are particularly prone to splitting where the grain of separate parts runs in different directions so the wood shrinks in different directions.**
Above **Splitting caused by rapid drying.**

Above and right **Splitting can be avoided in a large carving like this polar bear if the inside is hollowed out to leave the walls with an equal thickness.**

....

Instead, leave the wood until it has thoroughly dried and the inside of the carving has also shrunk. Many cracks will then reduce or even vanish altogether.

Wood can be assumed to be dry when it has been kept in the conditions in which it will finally live, and it stops losing weight. If filler must eventually be used, it should be no harder or more rigid than the wood around it.

Problems with unequal drying can also occur when one part of a carving is very heavy in relation to another part. If I have a carving with a flat base or back, I hollow out the wood so all parts have as equal a thickness as possible.

Even with a smaller solid shape such as a head it is advisable to drill and hollow it out as this allows the wood, which is then thinner, to move as temperature and humidity change. A solid lump cannot flex, so it splits.

GLUED JOINTS

Glued joints are strongest when the grain on both surfaces is parallel. The greater the difference in grain direction the weaker the joint will be. Joints on end grain are the weakest.

When carving wildlife, some people attach heads to bodies without any accurate joint, particularly when a painted finish is to be used which will cover joint lines.

What happens then is the wood shrinks but any resin used to fill the gap in the joint does not. Stress caused by this will eventually cause the joint to fail.

Some carvers try to prevent this by making the joint stronger with a dowel inserted down through the head into

the body. But if both head and body shrink the dowel can be pushed up through the top of the head. Alternatively, the head and body can separate, pushed apart by the dowel.

DOWELS

Dowels should be inserted from inside the carving, not drilled through from the outside, and room should be left around dowels to allow for the glue, and shrinkage of the surrounding wood.

....

How to dowel a joint.

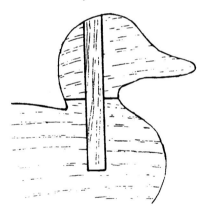

Wrong, the dowel is too tight and can be pushed out of the carving by shrinkage

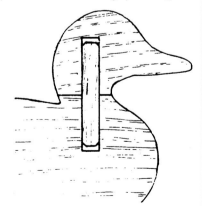

Right, space has been allowed for the glue and for shrinkage, and chamfered ends and grooves on the dowels help spread the glue

A dowel should not be too tight a fit or the glue will be scraped off it when it is pushed into place. Chamfers on the ends of dowels, and grooves cut along them, will help to spread the glue evenly, and allow air to escape from the joint as it is assembled.

Most dowelling sold by DIY stores is pine or ramin and quite unsuitable for carvers. I normally use beech dowels with straight grain. The strength across the grain is only about 5% of that with the grain.

GLUE

Glue will only stick wood directly to wood, it is not normally gap filling. Strength in a joint will probably halve if the gap is increased from two thousandths of an inch to four.

Any gap which is easily visible has little structural strength unless a gap-filling adhesive such as epoxy resin has been used.

If an epoxy resin must be used, such as when setting in glass eyes, a slow setting type should be used, as the shorter the setting time the greater will be the stress set up in the joint and the shorter its lifespan.

For decorative carvings it is best if the glue is water soluble. This will give future restorers a better chance of saving your work. While most non-soluble glues can be dissolved with chemicals, the wood around the glue is usually destroyed first.

SCREWS

It is best to avoid using steel screws for assembling carvings. Materials react differently to temperature and humidity, and while a steel screw will give a strong joint in the short term, in a hundred years time it may well have guaranteed the death of your creation.

Brass screws, although weaker, are much better. Drill the wood first using three drill sizes for thread, shank and head, and insert a steel screw to cut a thread in the wood. Then remove it

and replace it with an identical sized brass screw which has been rubbed with candle wax.

If you use a wooden plug to cover the screw head, make sure the grain runs in the same direction as the wood around it, which will ensure a few extra centuries of pleasure.

ABRASIVE STONES AND SANDING

Miniature grindstones can be used for smoothing wood before final finishing. These stones were developed for use in the metalworking industry. They cut steel because the hard metal constantly wears away the stone, exposing a new surface which continues cutting.

When used on wood, however, the resins in some woods can clog up the small holes in the stone. Ebony, for example, will clog a stone in just 30 seconds. The stone will then stop cutting and merely compress the surface of the wood.

Wood swells after sanding, and wood compressed by a stone may swell up months later. This can result in areas of the finish separating from the carving.

If I ever finish a carving by sanding I always wet it thoroughly after using the finest abrasive. When the wood is dry I then re-sand to remove the raised, swollen areas.

Miniature grinding stones can clog when used on wood. This one was clogged after 30 seconds use on ebony.

Section through wood.

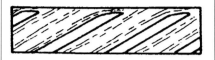

After sanding grain is compressed

After wetting grain is raised. When dry again this can be re-sanded to remove the raised area

The wood grain on this board was raised and swelled up after sanding.

FINISHING

Wood may not be as dry as the atmosphere into which a finished carving is placed, which results in the carving shrinking. If the finish is not securely bonded into the wood, the carving will be smaller than the finish surrounding it, and the finish will crack, bubble and flake.

The first layer of a finish must be diluted sufficiently to allow it to penetrate inside the wood, not just sit on the surface.

Penetration is almost exclusively through the end grain, so you can aid penetration by sanding at 45° to the grain to break the surface fibres. This is of course not practical where a polished finish is required, but helps with painted finishes.

Penetration of a finish is hindered by adhesives and most fillers, and also by stoning or sanding to a super smooth finish.

However, once a finish has penetrated inside the wood, subse-

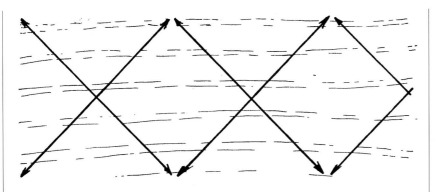

Above **Sand at 45° to the grain to break the surface fibres of wood before applying finish. This aids penetration.** Below **A finish can be seen penetrating the end grain of this board.**

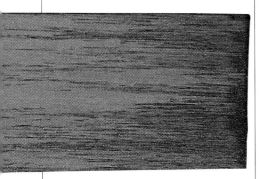

quent layers of a compatible finish will bond directly to the first layer.

If layers of finish do not bond to each other, there may be several reasons. Dust may not have been properly cleaned off after rubbing back the preceding coat. Oil, either natural oils from the wood or your skin when handling, may be forming a barrier. Different layers of finish may not be compatible with each other.

Each layer of finish should bond to the layer below, but problems can occur when the solvents involved are different. For example, a water-based sealer may be used before an alcohol-based polish.

If each layer does have a different solvent, then the lower layers should be slightly porous so the upper layers can soak into and bond directly to them, for example, gesso under paint or gold.

Where there are different solvents, or where the lower layer cures chemically before the next is applied, such as polyurethane, then sanding between coats increases the key and surface area and therefore the quality of bond.

Some finishes such as gesso are opaque and are applied to mask out the wood. Apart from these, some paints and most polishes are to some extent transparent or translucent. Light striking the carving will to some degree penetrate into the finish before being seen by the viewer.

If the finish is in one thick layer the

Below **Light reflects from each film of finish.**

result looks very treacly. The more layers, and the thinner the layers, the softer will be the effect. This is because the light will not be reflected from one point but from each individual film of finish.

If the final film of paint or polish appears harsh, the glazed effect can be muted by rubbing it with a very fine abrasive such as 0000 wire wool, followed by a wax polish, even over a painted surface. ●

Rod Naylor is a professional carver who works in a variety of styles from traditional to modern. He specialises in restoration work, mainly for museums and the National Trust. His work is in private and public collections around the world. Rod also works as a consultant for collectors, publishers and tool companies and produces work for other carvers. He designs, makes and sells carving equipment.

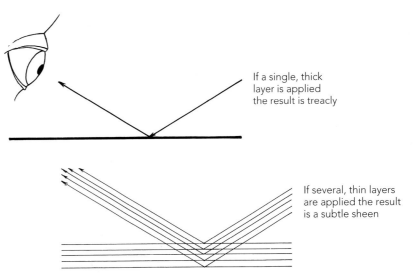

If a single, thick layer is applied the result is treacly

If several, thin layers are applied the result is a subtle sheen

PROJECT

MOTORBIKE MANTEL

**STEVE EGGLETON TELLS HOW HE
CARVED DECORATIVE MOTORCYCLE AND
FLAG SPANDRELS FOR THE ENTRANCE
TO A TIMBER-FRAMED COTTAGE**

someone of tender years however, be warned that lifting the seats of choir stalls in search of carved misericordes may involve you in some ticklish explanation, and not just about carving technique! The subject matter of these delightful carvings is often humorous, but also sometimes rather bawdy.

For me this grass roots 'nook and cranny' carving yields some of the most exciting work that can be found, and I see no reason why it should not continue. Today there are still plenty of possibilities for this sort of work, and we as woodcarvers need to actively promote the idea of decoration by relief carving.

When designing relief panels, it is often possible to divide them to present these opportunities. In my view, to approach these challenges with a sense of humour, tempered by an awareness of time and place, is entirely consistent with our heritage.

I was recently asked to make up an oak frame (*Quercus spp.*) for the arched door to a little timber-framed cottage in North Suffolk. The owner was a British motorcycle enthusiast, and wanted something appropriate carved in the spandrels of the frame.

The space was more or less triangular, so the designs had to lend themselves to this shape. As I played around with various ideas, I thought how brilliantly many such problems had been solved in the past.

FLEXIBLE DESIGN

I borrowed a pile of *British Motorcycling* magazines and suddenly found myself submerged in a sea of nostalgia. I recalled the early years of my marriage, when we had relied on an ancient AJS with sidecar for transport.

Dragging myself back to the present, I made a determined effort to find inspiration. Eventually I came up with the idea of a British flag for one corner and a motorcycle for the other. Clearly a square flag would not do. A triangular pennant

To be brought up as one of 12 in a tiny medieval woodcarver's cottage would be enough to give anyone a creative attitude towards cramped conditions. Was it this kind of 'spatially challenged' upbringing I wonder, that inspired our medieval brethren to have such fun with carving in the nooks and crannies of our old buildings?

The completed door in place

....

It is always worth taking time to wander round churches, cathedrals or early timber-framed buildings in search of these gems. Look up at the roof for the bosses and brackets from which the timbers spring.

If you are accompanied by

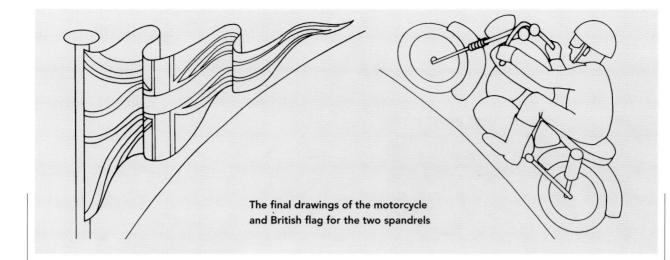

The final drawings of the motorcycle and British flag for the two spandrels

Top **Spandrel blanks. Note the sympathetic direction of the grain**
Centre and above **Transferring the designs using carbon paper. The two pins fixing the drawings are carefully placed in areas which will later be removed**

shape proved more appropriate.

Rejecting the idea of a chap in a racing pose, I found an upright riding position fitted more comfortably into the spandrel shape, although I had to adjust the shape of the wheels.

This slightly elliptical shape flowed better with the curve of the frame. At the same time, it gave the sense of a slightly oblique view, as if the machine was leaning over to take the bend.

This bending of the shape to suit the purposes of the task raises an interesting and age-old issue. In these days of cameras and computer generated designs we often forget that generations of woodcarvers, stonemasons and illuminators have been prepared to adjust their material to suit the needs presented by the job.

It is all too easy to view this flexibility of approach as primitive. It tends to give the impression that medieval people were either severely handicapped or brilliant contortionists!

Perhaps those who view our work in years to come may draw even more disturbing conclusions about us. We are probably too close to our own style and culture to discern this, rather like a man with a regional accent discerns nothing strange in his language or that of his native fellows.

RELIEF CARVING

Selecting timber for the carved spandrels was an important business, and when pricing a job you must always allow for the time and timber waste involved. To avoid short grain on the narrow ends of the spandrels, I selected blocks where the grain swung round the shape. I decided to make up the frame with the blank spandrels fitted, so the timber would be held securely for carving.

To match the window frames, I ran a bead up the frame posts and continued it round the arch. For this I used a simple scraper made up to match the bead. I keep the steel blades of old worn-out hand saws for this purpose. They make excellent scrapers and scratch-stock blades.

I transferred the designs to the timber with carbon paper, using a coloured ballpoint pen so I could see where I had been. Using a V-shaped gouge, I then cut round the outlines. I removed a depth of wood from the surrounding area, leaving each design

Above **Basic contours of the flag**
Below **Detail of the flag**

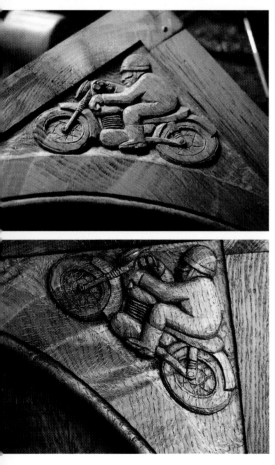

standing proud of its background. After cutting the outlines of the designs, I cleared the surrounding area away using a 7mm, ⁹⁄₃₂in shallow gouge.

The next stage involved shaping the basic contours, taking the work on that fascinating journey from two dimensions towards three. This conundrum of dimension is at the heart of relief carving, and it is important to challenge every flat surface. The contours were shaped using the same shallow gouge, and another favourite of mine, a 10mm ³⁄₈in flat gouge, but sharpened at an angle of about 10°.

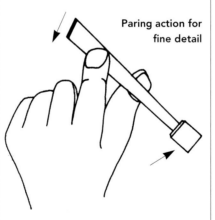

Paring action for fine detail

This has two advantages over a similar tool with a square end. First, it can reach into a corner more easily to leave a clean finish. Second, it works with a slicing rather than a planing action. Furthermore, when swung between the thumb and forefinger of the left hand, it is an efficient means of working the surface of a small area.

DETAIL

Having formed the contours of each shape, I put in the rest of the detail. I carved the detail with a small 1.5mm,

¹⁄₁₆in gouge and a fine pointed knife.

I used a range of different weighted mallets, according to the fineness of the work.

I made undercuts where possible to emphasise form, taking care to slope all top surfaces forwards so they shed moisture. This must always be a consideration where a carving has to stand outside in the weather.

The traditional outdoor treatment for oak is linseed oil, but it must be raw, as the boiled variety tends to skin over and dry like varnish, obscuring the carving. Adding a little oil-based colour to the oil accentuates the detail.

With age, oak tends to blacken, and dirt accumulates in all the crevices of the carved work. This only serves to improve the whole thing. To complete the job I designed some hinge-plates to match the motorcycling theme and fitted them using old reclaimed hand-made nails.

On returning to photograph the work it was a joy to watch the effect of these little carvings on passers-by. It is lovely to think of the people who will be cheered on their way by what is simply a rearrangement of contour. ●

Steve Eggleton trained as an art teacher at Portsmouth College of Education, and moved to Norfolk in 1975, where he has taught and worked as a woodcarver ever since. More recently his work in wood has extended to the making of musical instruments. Specialising in double-basses, he carves a face on each instrument instead of a scroll.

Top **Motorcyclist outlined with a V gouge**
Centre **Motorcyclist with detail**
Above **The motorcyclist after oiling. Note how the coloured oil accentuates the detail**

BONE IDOLS

IN THE FIRST OF TWO ARTICLES, SARAH HIPWELL TALKS TO CLIVE HALLAM ABOUT NETSUKE AND THE PREPARATION OF BONE FOR CARVING

Three years ago, I heard about some 'miniature sculptures', or netsuke, which Clive Hallam was carving in London. My curiosity abounded until Clive came to live in my home town of Dublin, giving me a golden opportunity to view them for myself.

Having seen these fascinating objects, I am writing this article to increase the awareness of netsuke and explain how an indigenous art form of Japan has achieved international interest.

It was not easy to find information about contemporary netsuke, so I am particularly grateful to Clive for sharing his time and knowledge with me.

ANCIENT ORIGINS

The most popular pronunciation of netsuke is *net-ski*, while the Japanese sounds closer to *net-skeh*, literally meaning root-attachment. Its origins go back about 300 years, when the traditional form of Japanese dress, the kimono, had no pockets.

Women would tuck small personal items into their sleeves, but men suspended their tobacco pouches, pipes, purses or writing implements on a silk cord from their sash (obi). The hanging objects were called Sagemono. To stop the cord from slipping through the obi, they attached a small toggle called a netsuke to it.

The netsuke is peculiar to Japan only in its native term. Devices with a similar function have been used in many other countries such as China, Tibet, Java, Africa, among the Eskimos and in Hungary.

But it is only in Japan that the toggle developed as a great art form. This is because of the national characteristic of the Japanese people to apply beauty to all aspects of their surroundings, even mundane utilitarian objects.

But during the period between 1875 and 1925, known as the Post Restoration or Meiji Period, the supply of great antique netsuke disappeared from Japan.

With a few exceptions, the next 50 years until around 1950 was a rather weak period in quality netsuke production. Mass produced or quickly executed, inexpensive netsuke were carved for export.

....

Netsuke in its traditional use

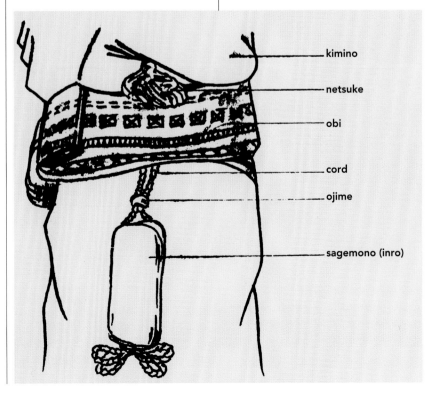

Fortunately by 1960, a whole new group of young, serious netsuke artists began to emerge. They were greatly encouraged by a small group of collectors who took great interest in their work and supported them with purchases. Books were also being written on the subject, and interest spread overseas.

There are about a hundred netsuke carvers in the world today, but only a handful are able to carve them as their sole profession. They are popular in America where there are a few carvers, plus one in Australia, two in England, a handful in Japan and Clive in Dublin.

DEFINING FEATURES

There are three essential characteristics of a netsuke. First, they must have two special holes (Himotoshi) through which the cord may pass. Carvings which do not have these holes (or an alternative) cannot be called netsuke and are known as Okimono, which means things to be displayed.

kimino

netsuke

obi

cord

ojime

sagemono (inro)

Top **Front view of a crab**
Above **Underside of a crab showing the hole through the centre through which the obi cord can pass**

A netsuke must be quite small, around 30mm, 1⅙in tall. It should be small enough to hold in your hands and pass beneath the obi. The last characteristic is it must be carved in the round, like dice, and carved on all sides.

CONTEMPORARY CARVER

Clive Hallam's background is in fine arts, specialising in large abstract paintings and metal sculpture. Although he was influenced by abstract impressionists, he became increasingly concerned with the social relevance of his work. He felt he had been communicating with a select audience, and his art was more about art than the world we live in.

So Clive started searching for a more personal, intimate art form which did not require a gallery or an elitist art establishment to be appreciated.

Clive believes the moment you take a piece of material and alter its form, the act of human intervention has turned it into a work of art, even if it's not a good work of art. He finds some form of discipline is essential and paradoxically finds the most freedom in the discipline of netsuke.

Netsuke is an art form which is

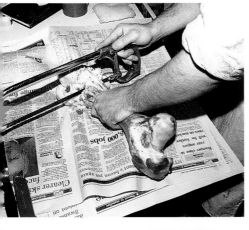

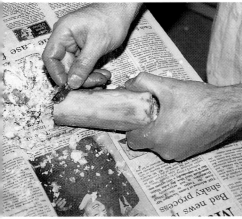

From top to bottom
- Initial cleaning of the cow bone
- Removing the ends of the bone so the marrow can be extracted
- Scraping the flesh from the cow bone
- Removing the bone marrow
- The cleaned bone is placed in hot water with bleach and washing up liquid

....

not earth bound to a plinth, it is suspended fully in the round. This explains why all netsuke are miniature sculptures, but not all miniature sculptures are netsuke.

CREATIVE PROCESS

There are certain structural limitations to netsuke which contributed towards creating an art form which is tactile and appreciated in the palm of your hand.

The traditional netsuke had to be compact. They were rounded and usually highly polished to protect them from their daily use as a toggle. Clive found them a big change from large scale painting and sculpture, as it was difficult to express himself in the slow process of carving.

The initial creative approach, however, was the same. "It involves me seeking subjects of personal interest in my environment and expressing myself through the use of drawing and other graphic mediums," Clive told me. Once he began to carve he had to embark upon an apprenticeship in carving techniques.

It was hard for Clive to get any guidance or literature on this unusual subject, so he used traditional antique netsuke carvings as examples, studying their craftsmanship and developing tools to create the same effects.

At the time he was unaware of any other contemporary carvers or that there was a market for netsuke. He developed his own techniques and made his own tools. After a few years, he met another netsuke carver in London and became aware of the contemporary netsuke scene. The

majority of carvers seemed to have learned through a similar process.

MATERIALS

Traditionally the Japanese netsuke carving technique was developed in ivory. But netsuke production decreased as the function became obsolete, and the ban on trade in endangered species polished off many traditional netsuke carvers who were unable to adapt to new materials. A few traditional carvers managed to develop their technique in wood.

The ban also gave rise to contemporary netsuke, as it broke the dominance of the Japanese carving tradition. Western carvers found the ban on ivory less of a problem as they were learning how to carve netsuke from scratch anyway. It gave people the opportunity to explore new materials, effectively creating a level playing field in terms of technical ability.

Clive has never used ivory himself, as he does not believe in creating one form of beauty by destroying another. He mainly uses boxwood (*Buxus sempervirens*) which is extremely dense and takes fine detailed carving. He also uses deer antler, and a number of different materials for inlay work, such as amber, coral and mother of pearl.

PREPARING BONE

Certain materials are better than others to achieve the required effect. For detailed realistic work, Clive prefers boxwood. But if he needs a more abstracted tactile effect, a material with an inherent variety of richness like antler is better.

Common cow bones can also be prepared to make a wonderful white and easily carved material. He showed me an example and the material looked luminous with an iridescent quality.

The best bone to use is the lower rear shank. First he cleaned off the flesh, and removed the marrow with a screwdriver. Then the bone was soaked in hot water to soften it.

Clive was careful not to let the hot water boil as that sets the blood in the bone and discolours it. First he added ½ a cup of detergent and ½ a cup of bleach and left the bone for two to three hours with the water kept hot.

Then he scraped the surface to remove all the waxy residue and any further marrow. The process was then repeated, soaking the bone for three to four hours after which it was rinsed and dried, standing up for not less than 24 hours. The bone was then ready to carve.

TACTILE STYLE

Clive doesn't see any difference between realistic and abstract styles, he sees them more as approaches to a subject. For example, he recently carved an owl, which was realistic because it had the anatomy of a bird.

More important was how it felt in the hand. Through subtle carving and simplicity of feather patterns, its tactile quality was softness, creating an impression of the quietness with which an owl flies. The realism hinted at the

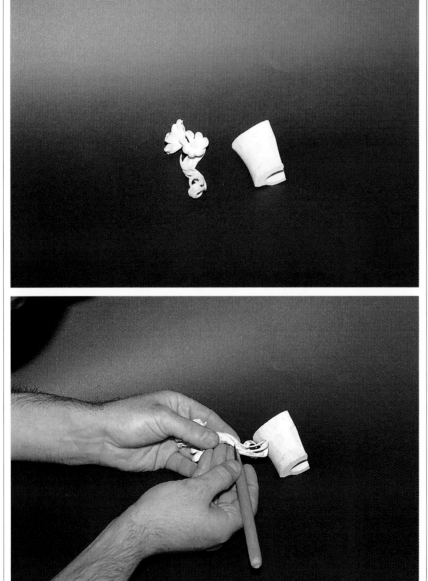

Above left **The prepared bone and a semi-finished netsuke made from cow's bone**
Left **Carving a netsuke, using a specially developed tool**
Top **For My Mother, carved in deer antler, depicts a mother owl protecting her young**
Above **Snail on Coke Can, A Tribute to Mitsuhiro, a playful contemporary parody on a traditional Japanese theme, in boxwood and lacquer**

INTIMATE ART

Clive and other new carvers are hoping to develop netsuke into the mainstream of contemporary art. Although there is no difference in the work itself, the scale is different. This gives the audience an intimacy with the work, sometimes lacking in other art forms.

The Sculptor Marcel Wolfers was quoted in the book *Fables in Ivory, Japanese Netsuke and their legends* (by Adrienne Barbanson), "Always available for handling, netsuke appeal first of all to the tactile sense. Their modelling, their charm, and their contrasts are appreciated by caressing them lovingly, and it is in this that the secret of their admirable patina lies."

It is also intriguing to witness a small block of wood being transformed from its natural state to take the shape of a creature or an abstract form. This once indigenous Japanese craft has been given a new life, in the shape of contemporary netsuke, which I hope will continue to grow.

In the next article Clive shows some of his techniques for creating his netsuke. ●

Clive Hallam was born in West Germany in 1965 and completed his degree in fine art at the University of Capetown in South Africa. Labelled an undesirable radical, Clive left South Africa in 1987 and travelled across Europe and Britain. He believes his lack of cultural identity contributed to his adoption of the netsuke art form. He is currently living in Dublin.

subject to be explored, while the abstract shapes and forms produced the desired emotional response.

Another example was a snail which was realistic in shape and appearance, but Clive also wanted to create a feeling of moistness on the body of the snail, while making the shell cold and hard.

The result was a realistic snail but it also had an essential 'snailness'. "This to me is abstraction, to abstract the essential nature of the subject," Clive explained. "The realism acts as a guide."

Further information

Oriental Art (Journal) Vol XL, Number 2, Summer 1994, pp 48–49

Fables in ivory, Japanese Netsuke and their legends
Adrienne Barbanson, Tuttle, Tokyo and Rutland, Vermont, 1961

Collector's Netsuke
Raymond Bushnell, Weatherhill New York and Tokyo, 1971

The Art of Netsuke Carving by Masatoshi as told to Raymond Bushell
Kodansha International, Tokyo, New York and San Francisco 1981

Netsuke
Neil Davey, Faber & Faber, London, in association with Sotheby Parke Bernet Publications, 1974

An introduction to Netsuke
Joe Earle, Victoria and Albert Museum, London, 1980

Contemporary Netsuke
Miriam Kinsey, Tuttle, Tokyo and Rutland, Vermont, 1997

The Art of the Netsuke Carver
Frederick Meinertzhagen, Routledge and Kegan Paul, London, 1956

Netsuke, Masterpieces from the Metropolitan Museum of Art
Barbra Teri Okada, Metropolitan Museum of Art, New York, 1982

Netsuke, The miniature sculpture of Japan
Richard Barker and Lawrence Smith, British Museum Publications Ltd, 1976

Annual Catalogues on Contemporary Netsuke
Michael Spindel, Seaford, New York

TECHNIQUE

SMALL WONDERS

IN THE SECOND OF TWO ARTICLES, SARAH HIPWELL DISCOVERS MORE OF CLIVE HALLAM'S TECHNIQUES FOR CARVING NETSUKE

The basic design for the tool resembles a hooked knife. He makes them himself using high carbon steel. Although he finds shaping the tools straightforward, tempering the cutting point of such a small piece of metal can be tricky. The tool is fixed with a pencil-thin handle, and is pivoted on the thumb.

Netsuke carving is a highly specialised occupation. The intricate nature of the work has led to the development of remarkable techniques. As an international carver, Clive Hallam uses a number of approaches, some Japanese and some of the more traditional western techniques.

I visited him at his Dublin workshop hoping to gain an insight into the process of carving these small sculptures and was pleasantly surprised at how open Clive was about discussing his techniques.

In roughing the basic shape of a netsuke, he uses standard western methods. A dental drill or similar hobby flexishaft with small burrs is great for roughing out.

The final detail requires more control. Clive explained he does not so much carve, as scrape the shapes, using traditional Japanese designs for tools.

Above **Clive used the *ukibori* technique to create the pimple effect on the snail body**
Below ***Snail On Coke Can*, in lacquer over boxwood (*Buxus sempervirens*)**

The pivoted action gives great control over the cutting edge. The hooked shape of the tool can be adapted to reach inaccessible places.

PRODUCING PIMPLES

One of the methods Clive has discovered is producing tiny raised characters such as the pimples on the side of the small snail on the Cola can. I was amazed at the sight of 40–50 tiny pimples on an area not much bigger than my thumb nail. Each pimple seemed individually carved with perfect uniformity. It looked as if it had taken months of work.

Clive explained the principle behind this technique called *ukibori*, which can be adapted to produce all manner of effects. For example you could also produce the effect of a snake's scales or raised letters to produce tiny inscriptions.

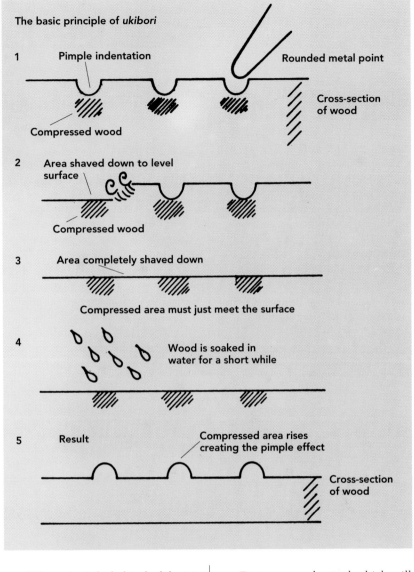

The basic principle of *ukibori*

1   Pimple indentation   Rounded metal point

Compressed wood

Cross-section of wood

2   Area shaved down to level surface

Compressed wood

3   Area completely shaved down

Compressed area must just meet the surface

4   Wood is soaked in water for a short while

5   Result   Compressed area rises creating the pimple effect

Cross-section of wood

Top **A selection of scraper tools Clive uses for netsuke carving**
Centre **Using a scraper tool to carve a netsuke**
Above **A special tool is needed to make the indentations for the *ukibori* technique**

"The principle behind *ukibori* is simple, but this technique should only be used as a tool in creative expression and not as a special effect to dazzle the viewer," Clive told me.

First you need a tool which will produce the desired depression. This should have a thin shaft and rounded metal point which will make a small indentation in the wood surface,

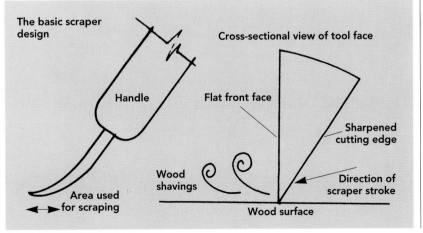

The basic scraper design

Cross-sectional view of tool face

Handle

Flat front face

Sharpened cutting edge

Wood shavings

Direction of scraper stroke

Area used for scraping

Wood surface

compressing the wood at the pit of the depression.

When the indentations have been created, the area is shaved down to a level surface. The compressed area should just meet the surface. Then the wood is soaked in water for a short while, after which the compressed area rises, giving a pimple effect.

AMBER EYES

A difficult but impressive technique is the carving of amber eyes for animals and birds. The technique is called *happonirami*, literally meaning staring in eight directions.

The technique creates the effect of the eyes following the viewer from whichever angle the face is seen. Amber eyes do not have to be perfectly round but can be customised to suit, perhaps taking the eye lids into account.

I watched Clive prepare an eye for a bird he carved. He began by preparing a long cylinder of clear amber. Then he made a shallow cylindrical cavity in the carving and matched its size to the amber, constantly checking until the amber fitted tightly and perfectly to the bird's head. He then painted the cavity base with a dab of yellow paint, putting the bird away to dry.

Using a hobby drill and very fine dental burr he carved a shallow depression in the flat top of the cylinder of amber. He then cleaned and polished the depression using a sliver of willow and a car polish called Autosol. Clive tells me it is freely available and for polishing it's hard to beat.

When finished, the cavity was filled with Indian ink. Clive added a dot of Superglue when the ink had dried to seal it. He then glued the whole cylinder into the cavity on the bird.

Once dry, he carefully cut the protruding cylinder and using his tiny knives, scraped the eye into a dome. The shape of the dome had to be perfectly round as it would have the effect of magnifying the pupil created by the ink. He then polished the eye in a similar way to the pupil depression. The effect really gave a feeling of life to the bird.

Clive's open attitude to sharing his techniques was remarkable considering the amount of effort he has made to gain this knowledge for himself. But as he pointed out, "the technique itself is not precious, but only the quality of its execution." ●

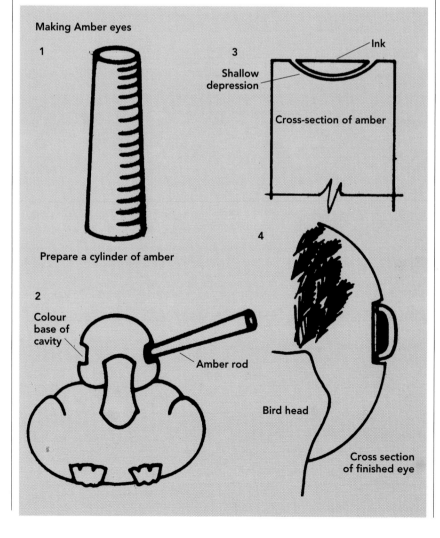

Making Amber eyes

1

Prepare a cylinder of amber

2

Colour base of cavity

Amber rod

3

Ink

Shallow depression

Cross-section of amber

4

Bird head

Cross section of finished eye

Clive Hallam was born in West Germany in 1965 and completed his degree in fine art at the University of Capetown in South Africa. Labelled an undesirable radical, Clive left South Africa in 1987 and travelled across Europe and Britain. He believes his lack of cultural identity contributed to his adoption of the netsuke art form. He is currently living in Dublin.

PROJECT MASCOT IN MDF

JIM HEATH EXPLAINS HOW HE CARVED A WELSH DRAGON FOR A FIBREBOARD MANUFACTURER

The finished dragon

I carved the Kronospan dragon as a result of approaching the company to sponsor me to do some work in MDF (Medium Density Fibreboard). The Kronospan factory in Chirk is one of the biggest MDF and chipboard manufacturing plants in Europe and attracts a lot of bad press from local environmentalists.

Having just started my own business under the Enterprise Allowance Scheme, I wanted as much publicity as I could get, and thought getting sponsorship from them would bring good publicity to both of us. They had a major trade show coming up and commissioned the dragon for the centrepiece of their display.

I drew the outline of the dragon onto tracing paper and sub-divided it into various component shapes. I transferred the shapes to 4ft square, 1200mm pieces of 1¼in, 30mm MDF using carbon paper.

Then I cut the shapes out using a jig-saw. I needed 30 separate pieces to give the required proportions. My 10-year-old handyman jig-saw packed up half way through the second piece, so I finished the job with a hired one.

ASSEMBLY

I clamped the components together dry to check the proportions were right and the general shape worked. Since the dragon had one leg raised, I also checked it would actually stand up. At this stage it became clear just how heavy the finished article would be.

My next step was to glue the components together to form three sections. I joined the left hand body with the legs and wing, the right hand body with the legs and wing and the body mid-section with the neck and head.

Part-way through this stage I decided it would be easier to carve the

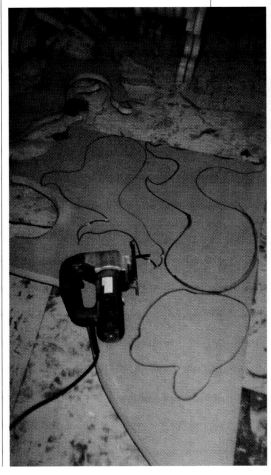

Cutting out the components

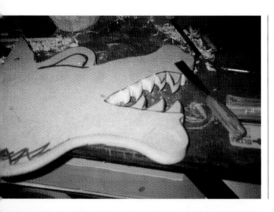

teeth and tongue before assembling the head section. I assembled the sections over three consecutive days, as each one used my entire stock of clamps and cramps. I used PVA adhesive and did the roughing out with an Arbortech disk.

The reason I assembled the three separate sections rather than the whole job was two-fold. First it was easier to manoeuvre the pieces out into the garden and back, and second I could move around each of the legs, the head

and both sides of each wing. I did the final assembly after roughing out, again using PVA adhesive and every available cramp and clamp.

LAST CUTS

I got down to the final carving with a range of traditional gouges, taking care to work with the material rather than against it. Although MDF has no grain, the method of construction creates layering, which means if you cut in one

Top **Carving the teeth before assembly**

Above **Assembly of the left hand body section**

direction you get a clean finish, and if you cut in the opposite direction you get a tearing effect. I also had to be careful not to make the wood too thin, as the structure would become fragile.

Below left **The dragon fully assembled ready for carving**

FINISHING

I sanded the wings, breast scales and eyes to produce a smooth finish and left the rest of the dragon with a gouge finish. I then gave the whole carving a liberal coating of beeswax and turpentine. I chose beeswax because it had no effect on the natural colour of the MDF.

Most other finishes would have darkened it, which might have detracted from the purpose of promoting the product.

The result was a Welsh dragon 6ft x 4ft6in x 20in, 183 x 136 x 51cm. The trade show for which it was commissioned was the world's biggest furniture show held in Singapore. ●

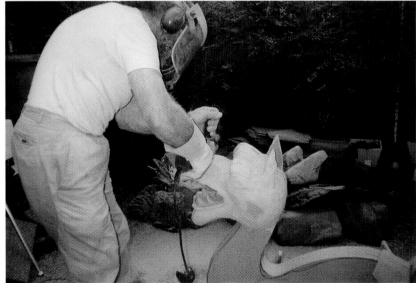

Top right
and above
**Jim roughs
out with an
Arbortech disk**

Jim Heath lives in Chirk, North Wales. He is known for his wildlife carvings, some of which formed part of Wildlife Art '95, an exhibition of wildlife sculpture and painting held in Berkampstead, Hertfordshire last summer.

INDEX

GMC PUBLICATIONS

BOOKS

WOODTURNING

Adventures in Woodturning	David Springett	Practical Tips for Turners & Carvers	GMC Publications
Bert Marsh: Woodturner	Bert Marsh	Practical Tips for Woodturners	GMC Publications
Bill Jones' Notes from the Turning Shop	Bill Jones	Spindle Turning	GMC Publications
Bill Jones' Further Notes from the Turning Shop	Bill Jones	Turning Miniatures in Wood	John Sainsbury
Carving on Turning	Chris Pye	Turning Wooden Toys	Terry Lawrence
Colouring Techniques for Woodturners	Jan Sanders	Understanding Woodturning	Ann & Bob Phillips
Decorative Techniques for Woodturners	Hilary Bowen	Useful Woodturning Projects	GMC Publications
Faceplate Turning: Features, Projects, Practice	GMC Publications	Woodturning: A Foundation Course	Keith Rowley
Green Woodwork	Mike Abbott	Woodturning Jewellery	Hilary Bowen
Illustrated Woodturning Techniques	John Hunnex	Woodturning Masterclass	Tony Boase
Keith Rowley's Woodturning Projects	Keith Rowley	Woodturning: A Source Book of Shapes	John Hunnex
Make Money from Woodturning	Ann & Bob Phillips	Woodturning Techniques	GMC Publications
Multi-Centre Woodturning	Ray Hopper	Woodturning Wizardry	David Springett
Pleasure & Profit from Woodturning	Reg Sherwin		

WOODCARVING

The Art of the Woodcarver	GMC Publications	Understanding Woodcarving	GMC Publications
Carving Birds & Beasts	GMC Publications	Wildfowl Carving Volume 1	Jim Pearce
Carving Realistic Birds	David Tippey	Wildfowl Carving Volume 2	Jim Pearce
Carving on Turning	Chris Pye	The Woodcarvers	GMC Publications
Decorative Woodcarving	Jeremy Williams	Woodcarving: A Complete Course	Ron Butterfield
Essential Woodcarving Techniques	Dick Onians	Woodcarving for Beginners: Projects, Techniques & Tools	
Lettercarving in Wood	Chris Pye		GMC Publications
Practical Tips for Turners & Carvers	GMC Publications	Woodcarving Tools, Materials & Equipment	Chris Pye

PLANS, PROJECTS, TOOLS & THE WORKSHOP

The Incredible Router	Jeremy Broun	Sharpening Pocket Reference Book	Jim Kingshott
Making & Modifying Woodworking Tools	Jim Kingshott	The Workshop	Jim Kingshott
Sharpening: The Complete Guide	Jim Kingshott		

TOYS & MINIATURES

Designing & Making Wooden Toys	Terry Kelly	Making Wooden Toys & Games	Jeff & Jennie Loader
Fun to Make Wooden Toys & Games	Jeff & Jennie Loader	Miniature Needlepoint Carpets	Janet Granger
Making Board, Peg & Dice Games	Jeff & Jennie Loader	Turning Miniatures in Wood	John Sainsbury
Making Little Boxes from Wood	John Bennett	Turning Wooden Toys	Terry Lawrence

CREATIVE CRAFTS

Celtic Knotwork Designs	Sheila Sturrock	Embroidery Tips & Hints	Harold Hayes
Collage from Seeds, Leaves and Flowers	Joan Carver	Making Knitwear Fit	Pat Ashforth & Steve Plummer
The Complete Pyrography	Stephen Poole	Miniature Needlepoint Carpets	Janet Granger
Creating Knitwear Designs	Pat Ashforth & Steve Plummer	Tatting Collage	Lindsay Rogers
Cross Stitch on Colour	Sheena Rogers		

UPHOLSTERY AND FURNITURE

Care & Repair	*GMC Publications*	Making Shaker Furniture	*Barry Jackson*
Complete Woodfinishing	*Ian Hosker*	Pine Furniture Projects	*Dave Mackenzie*
Furniture Projects	*Rod Wales*	Seat Weaving (Practical Crafts)	*Ricky Holdstock*
Furniture Restoration (Practical Crafts)	*Kevin Jan Bonner*	Upholsterer's Pocket Reference Book	*David James*
Furniture Restoration & Repair for Beginners	*Kevin Jan Bonner*	Upholstery: A Complete Course	*David James*
Green Woodwork	*Mike Abbott*	Upholstery: Techniques & Projects	*David James*
Making Fine Furniture	*Tom Darby*	Woodfinishing Handbook (Practical Crafts)	*Ian Hosker*

DOLLS' HOUSES & DOLLS' HOUSE FURNITURE

Architecture for Dolls' Houses	*Joyce Percival*	Making Period Dolls' House Accessories	*Andrea Barham*
A Beginners' Guide to the Dolls' House Hobby	*Jean Nisbett*	Making Period Dolls' House Furniture	*Derek & Sheila Rowbottom*
The Complete Dolls' House Book	*Jean Nisbett*	Making Victorian Dolls' House Furniture	*Patricia King*
Easy-to-Make Dolls' House Accessories	*Andrea Barham*	Miniature Needlepoint Carpets	*Janet Granger*
Make Your Own Dolls' House Furniture	*Maurice Harper*	The Secrets of the Dolls' House Makers	*Jean Nisbett*
Making Dolls' House Furniture	*Patricia King*		

OTHER BOOKS

Guide to Marketing	*GMC Publications*	Woodworkers' Career & Educational Source Book	*GMC Publications*

VIDEOS

Carving a Figure: The Female Form	*Ray Gonzalez*	Woodturning: A Foundation Course	*Keith Rowley*
The Traditional Upholstery Workshop		Elliptical Turning	*David Springett*
Part 1: *Drop-in & Pinstuffed Seats*	*David James*	Woodturning Wizardry	*David Springett*
The Traditional Upholstery Workshop		Turning Between Centres: The Basics	*Dennis White*
Part 2: *Stuffover Upholstery*	*David James*	Turning Bowls	*Dennis White*
Hollow Turning	*John Jordan*	Boxes, Goblets & Screw Threads	*Dennis White*
Bowl Turning	*John Jordan*	Novelties & Projects	*Dennis White*
Sharpening Turning & Carving Tools	*Jim Kingshott*	Classic Profiles	*Dennis White*
Sharpening the Professional Way	*Jim Kingshott*	Twists & Advanced Turning	*Dennis White*

MAGAZINES

WOODTURNING • WOODCARVING • TOYMAKING
FURNITURE & CABINETMAKING • BUSINESSMATTERS
• CREATIVE IDEAS FOR THE HOME

The above represents a full list of all titles currently published or scheduled to be published. All are available direct from the Publishers or through bookshops, newsagents and specialist retailers. To place an order, or to obtain a complete catalogue, contact:

GMC Publications, 166 High Street, Lewes, East Sussex BN7 1XU United Kingdom
Tel: 01273 488005 Fax: 01273 478606

Orders by credit card are accepted